# Prophetic Ministry

Ron McKenzie

Kingwatch Books

Kingwatch Books
Christchurch
New Zealand
www.kingwatch.co.nz

# Contents

## Acknowledgement

Over the years, I have searched out every book and article that has been written about the prophetic ministry. The best gems from these are included in this book. Many more can be found at www.kingwatch.co.nz/Prophet.htm.

## Cover Picture

Most people focus on things close at hand. Some see the beauty of the autumn colours, while others just see decaying leaves. Prophets look ahead and see the living waters of the Holy Spirit at work. A few look into the distance and see the mountain of God's Kingdom filling the earth.

# 1

# Prophetic Voice

## Clear Vision

Lack of vision and direction limits the modern church. Many Christians just go from fad to fad, with nothing followed through to completion. Many churches have to obtain a vision by copying other successful churches.

The Bible says that without a vision the people will perish (Prov 29:18). A dearth of prophets has caused a lack of vision in the church. Paul says,

> If the trumpet does not give a clear call, who will get ready
> for battle (1 Cor 14:8).

The church needs prophets to give a clear call to battle. It is currently losing the battle because it does not have a focused strategy. A great babble of voices all claim to have the truth and Christians are tossed around by every new wave that comes along. A clear prophetic voice is needed to prepare the church for victory.

Being without prophets is a sign that a people are under a curse.

> We are given no miraculous signs; no prophets are left, and
> none of us knows how long this will be (Ps 74:9).

*We presently have little or no understanding of the ultimate and full purposes of God in and through His people. The church is bored stiff, lacking an orbit, a line of thought and a direction because it lacks this understanding. We condemn ourselves, therefore, to programs and services whose forms are unhappily predictable (Art Katz - What is the Prophetic Church).*

*The prophet sees the sweep and the purpose of God, the larger picture, the panoramic view. He is not one for the 'nuts and bolts', for the details: 'how do you do this and that'. He sees the arching overview, and that is what the church needs to see if that is the framework of its life. Without that overview, fellowships will be fixed entirely in the present moment. They will remain in the things that are really so narrow and so petty because they cannot see what they are doing and what they are about in this moment in the context of something much larger of which they are in connection and moving toward. Without the prophetic overview, they are caught up in the immediate program, which very likely has been birthed out of their flesh or out of a necessity to 'do something', and is not consciously in the continuum of things apostolic and prophetic (T. Austin-Sparks - What is Prophetic Ultimacy)?*

## Restoration of the Prophetic

The most urgent need of the modern church is for the restoration of the prophetic ministry. In recent years, the gift of prophecy has been rediscovered, but there is still a desperate shortage of prophets. The church will not come to true maturity until prophets are being raised up among God's people.

Unfortunately, the role of the prophetic ministry has caused disagreement in the church. Some writers have suggested that the role of the Old Testament prophets ended with the cross. They believe that New Testament prophets are limited to encouragement and exhortation. This view turns prophets into Good News Guys.

Many church leaders fear the prophetic. They are happy for prophetic people to give personal words to people during church services, but want the leadership of the church to be immune from prophetic challenge. This has truncated an important ministry and weakened the church. The quality of the prophets is critical for building the body of Christ on a solid foundation (Eph 2:20), so we need to understand how the ministry of Jesus changed their role.

## Old Testament Prophets

The common belief is that Old Testament prophets were old men with beards, who went around speaking doom and gloom, but this is a misleading caricature. The main role of the prophets was to speak for God. In Old Testament times, the Holy Spirit had not been poured out on God's people, so only a few people operated under the anointing of the Spirit. Most people could not hear the Spirit speaking, so they needed someone to tell them what God was saying.

A key part of the prophetic role was to watch over the covenant. Whenever, Israel broke the covenant, the prophets would challenge them and warn of the consequence. Israel broke the covenant over and over again, which is why the prophets seemed to be full of doom and gloom. Israel was mostly in disobedience, so the prophets spent most of their time warning of the consequence of this disobedience. They could not be nice, because the prognosis for Israel was usually nasty.

A minor role of the more mature prophets was to speak to the nations around Israel. God raises them up and brings them down to accomplish purposes. Isaiah, Jeremiah and Ezekiel prophesied to nations like Egypt and Babylon. They did not speak to these nations in terms of the covenant, because they were not under it. However, these nations were created by God, so they are accountable to him. The prophets warned that if they slipped too far into evil, God would have to bring them down. However, speaking to the other nations was a minor part of the prophet's role.

Christians often assume that words of the Old Testament prophets were perfect and had to be obeyed without question. This is not true. The scriptures contain the prophet's best words. They were preserved, because the community assessed these words to be true and reliable. Those that were wrong were quickly forgotten, so we do not have access to them. The Old Testament prophets could make mistakes. Samuel was wrong in some of the things he did. Elisha got things wrong too. One prophet deliberately lied (1 Kings 13:18).

## New Covenant

The cross and resurrection of Jesus did not cause the role of the prophet to cease. Agabus, Judas and Silas are described as prophets in the New Testament, so the ministry continued (Acts 11:28; Acts 15:32). There is no indication that any aspect of the role has been fulfilled or ended.

Several things have changed. In Old Testament times, Israel was the people of the covenant. In New Testament times, the church is the people of the new covenant. The prophetic role of watching over the covenant continues, but the focus shifted to the new covenant and the church. The prophets are still responsible for watching over the church and warning if it breaks the covenant of Jesus. This is not a doom and gloom ministry, because in contrast to Israel, the victory of the cross and the spirit means that the church mostly walks in blessing.

There will be times when a church leaves God's path and needs to be challenged by a prophet. John's letters to the seven churches are examples of a prophetic challenge to a church that had lost the plot. These warnings to the church should not be required too often, if it is walking in the Spirit.

One of the greatest threats to the New Testament church is persecution. The role of the New Testament prophets includes responsibility for encouraging the church through times of persecution and suffering. John's letters to the seven churches are an example of this (Rev 3:21).

The role of prophesying to the people of the old covenant has been curtailed by the cross. Jesus himself gave the final prophesy to Israel when warning of the destruction of Jerusalem (Matt 23:33-24:2). He declared that Israel would not get a prophetic word again for a long, long time.

> Look, your house is left to you desolate. For I tell you, you will not see me again until you say, "Blessed is he who comes in the name of the Lord" (Matt 23:38-39).

Being left without prophets is part of their desolation. All future prophets will be followers of Jesus, so if the Jews will not accept those who come in his name, they will have no prophets (Micah 3:6). New Testament prophets will only get to speak freely to Israel when the Times of the Gentiles are coming to an end.

The role of prophesying to the other nations continues in New Testament times. God continues to determine the rising and falling of the nations.

> He made all the nations…; and he marked out their appointed times in history and the boundaries of their lands (Acts 17:26).

When nations go sour, God often lets them collapse and die. His role in this is clearer, if prophets explain to the collapsing nation why it is falling apart. This role has been lacking for a long time, so it needs to be restored.

Prophetic proclamation is the best way to remove a bad government. The Old Testament prophets brought down kings and rulers who had lost their way. For example, Elijah's prophetic work led to the destruction of Ahab. Daniel prophesied the fall of Belshazzar of Babylon. John continued this role in the New Testament by prophesying of the fall of Babylon the Great. We need to see more of this ministry from prophets in the New Testament age. If a Christian prophet had pronounced judgement against Saddam Hussein, releasing the power of God to remove him from office, his fall would have been far less painful for the Iraqi people than a ten-year war.

Speaking to the nations is only a minor aspect of the prophetic role, so only a few very mature prophets will be called to the role of prophet to the nations. Most New Testament prophets will function within the church. Some will grow to be a prophet to their own nation, and a few of these will emerge as prophets to other nations.

## Everyone can Prophecy

The cross and resurrection brought another major change. On the day of Pentecost, the Holy Spirit was poured out on everyone who believed. This changed everything, because every Christian can now hear the Holy Spirit speak. We no longer need a special group of people to tell us what God is saying. This shrinks the role of the prophets, because I do not need a prophet to tell me where to find my donkeys (1 Sam 10:2). If I need guidance about what to do, I should be able to hear the voice of the Spirit myself.

The other effect of the outpouring of the Spirit is that every Christian can prophesy. Peter explained this on the day of Pentecost.

> I will pour out my Spirit on all people.
> Your sons and daughters will prophesy (Acts 2:17).

This general ability to prophesy manifests in the gift of prophecy (1 Cor 12:10). With prophecy becoming more prevalent and widespread, the risk of poor quality prophecy is increased. This is why Paul gave clear guidance to the Corinthians about how this gift can be managed in a way that minimises harm. 1 Corinthians 14 is not a re-definition of the role of the prophet as some writers have claimed. Rather, it provides guidelines on how prophecy should be managed in a situation where everyone, including young people, can prophesy. Paul suggests that people should take turns in prophesying to keep the process orderly. He also encourages the church to test all prophecies, and discard those that are faulty (1 Thes 5:19-22).

Paul's letters focus on testing prophecies, not testing people. There is no test that has to be met before someone can exercise the gift of prophecy, because this gift is available to everyone. On the other hand, because the gift is so open, it is necessary to test every prophetic word spoken to sort the chaff from the wheat.

## Gift of Prophecy and the Ministry of the Prophet

The gift of prophecy is for edification and encouragement to build up the church (1 Cor 14:3). It is not for admonition and correction. That responsibility is kept for the prophets, because it is harder to speak challenging words without being harsh or proud.

*It takes humility to know the difference between prophecy and exhortation. Exhortation is not prophecy (Mario Murillo - Prophecy).*

Prophets are subject to a tough character test, because they are in a role that can do great harm, if they are insecure or weak. Jesus said that we would know the true prophets by the fruit of their service in their church. It takes time for fruit to emerge (Matt 7:15-20).

Every church will need admonition and correction from time to time. Therefore, every church should have at least one person who is recognized and established in this role. These prophets must not be constrained to comfort prophecies by 1 Corinthians 14:3. They must be free to say whatever God wants said to the church, with the only constraint being to speak the truth in love.

11

The gift of prophecy in the church is given by the Spirit for the encouragement and edification of believers. It is a gift that is available to all believers and any believer can experience it. In fact we are told that we should all earnestly seek the gift of prophecy (1 Cor 14:1,3). However, not everyone who prophesies is a prophet.

> *You can have spiritual gifting and insight, but that does not mean God has set you in a position of governing authority. God gives gifts to men by His Spirit, but the governing offices are established by the Lord Jesus. We get into trouble when we mistake gifts for offices (John Bevere - Thus Saith the Lord).*

The ministry of the prophet is an eldership ministry and a calling from God. A prophet is an elder called to speak the word of God, as spokesperson. Whereas the gift of prophecy can be given to any believer as the Spirit wills, the ministry of the prophet is a calling.

In practice, there will be a continuum of gifting. Some people will give an occasional prophecy (this is where most prophets begin). Others may prophesy more frequently. Some people who are appointed as elders may be just beginning in the prophetic. Others elders may have developed into a fuller prophetic ministry. The main goal is for all Christians to develop into their calling. We should not constrain people by trying to put precise labels on them. They should be free to be what God wants them to be.

## Robust Prophets

The gift of prophecy has brought blessing to the church, but much of the prophecy that is given is too tame. Paul said:

> If an unbeliever or someone who does not understand comes in while everybody is prophesying, he will be convinced by all that he is a sinner and will be judged by all, and the secrets of his heart will be laid bare. So he will fall down and worship God, exclaiming, "God is really among you" (1 Cor 14:24-25).

Prophecy with this power is rare in the church. Jeremiah said that the word of the Lord is like fire, or like a hammer that breaks a rock in pieces (Jer 23:29). The church will only experience powerful prophesying, when prophets are given their proper place in the church.

The restoration of the prophetic ministry is essential for the vitality of the church. Whereas the gift of prophecy can be given to any believer as the Spirit wills, the ministry of the prophet is a calling on a person's life. The church urgently needs this ministry.

> *There is a power in prophecy, which nothing can stand against (Anne Van Niekerk).*

## Prophets in the Church

Most prophets will function in the context of the church. A prophet is just an elder who sees things in black and white. They will ask the tough questions and challenge church members with besetting sins. A prophet is really an elder, who has a passion for truth and righteousness.

Each church should be led by a team of elders (Acts 14:23). The minimum number of elders would be three or four. They should work together by submitting to each other (Acts 13:1). The elders will be linked together by their commitment to each other. The relationships between them are the strength of the church.

Paul describes the role of elders in his letter to the Ephesians. Their role is to build up the body of Christ to maturity. There are four different functions that are necessary for this to happen.

> He gave some to be apostles, some to be prophets, some to be evangelists, and some to be pastors and teachers, to prepare God's people for works of service, so that the body of Christ may be built up until we all reach unity in the faith and in the knowledge of the Son of God (Eph 4:11-13).

Building up the body of Christ is the responsibility of elders, so these gifts are different tasks that elders do. An elder can be an apostle, a prophet, an evangelist, or a pastor-teacher. Each elder will fulfil one of these functions, according to the gifts that Christ has given. All of these ministries should be represented in the church eldership. One of these elders will be a prophet. One will be an evangelist. Several will be pastor-teachers.

Prophets, evangelists and pastors are elders with different giftings. Having all these ministries present in the eldership gives balance to the church. Without this balance, the church will not grow to maturity and unity. The prophet will provide vision for the church and keep it on the right track by ensuring that there is an emphasis on holiness. A prophet is really an elder who challenges the church and gives vision.

## Strong Foundation

The prophetic ministry is a fundamental aspect of the eldership. Without a prophet, a church will be weak in vision and at risk of sinfulness. The reason we have so many immature and weak churches is that prophets are missing from their leadership. Likewise, without an evangelist the church will not grow.

The main reason that the prophetic ministry is not functioning in the modern church is that most churches are led by a pastor-leader, so most prophets have had to become pastors to find a place of ministry. This is not a solution, because the church operates best when elders are functioning in their true ministry and not trying to be something they are not.

All of the ascension ministries of leadership are needed for a church to grow to maturity. The prophetic ministry must be part of the foundation of the church. Without a prophet, a church will be prone to sin. A strong church needs the righteousness that only comes when prophets are present. The modern church has millions of pastors, but only a few prophets. This serious imbalance has severely weakened the body of Christ.

## Assured Prophets

Every church needs at least one assured prophet. Sometimes it can be difficult to test a prophecy, because the message given is rather general. The prophecy may be biblically correct, but it may not be what God is actually saying at the time. It is more fruitful to test prophets. They can be watched over a period of time to see if their lives bear fruit. Jesus said that good fruit is the best test of a prophet.

> *The prophet bears a responsibility to place himself continually in the presence of God seeking to hear the word of the Lord and asking the Lord for guidance and direction, for encouragement or rebuke. When the Christian community needs guidance, it can rightly look to its prophets for a word from the Lord (Bruce Yocum - Prophecy).*

A false prophet will become obvious through the damage that follows their ministry (Matt 7:15-20). Every church needs a prophet, who is known to have a true ministry, and can be relied upon to speak the word of the Lord when it is needed.

Many of the spiritual gifts required can be manifested in other church members, but the ascension gifts must be manifested in the eldership of a church. One person cannot exercise all these ministries. A church needs all the gifts of eldership, especially prophets.

## Apostles and Prophets

The church is built on the foundation of the apostles and prophets. A building with a faulty foundation will eventually collapse.

An apostle is an elder sent out to establish a new church. The Greek word "apostlos" literally means one who is sent.

It is applied to a messenger who is sent on a mission. In the New Testament, it is used to describe a person who is sent out to establish a new church. When starting a new church, apostles will normally move into the next neighbourhood or village. They will go where the Spirit is moving, so hearing God's voice will be important in knowing where to go.

An apostle should always be accompanied by a prophet. Barnabas (Acts 4:36) and Silas (Acts 15:32) were prophets who accompanied Paul. When Paul and Barnabas had a disagreement, Paul was not prepared to go out until he had found another prophet (Silas) to go with him.

An apostolic team should also include an evangelist. Timothy (2 Tim 4:5) and Mark were evangelists who accompanied Paul. The evangelist would have specific responsibility for sharing the gospel.

The most experienced prophet should be sent out with the apostle, because starting the new church is the most demanding task. Good prophetic insight must be part of the church from the beginning, so it will be built on a foundation of righteousness and holiness. Every new work must be based on a clear vision. When a prophet is absent from the apostolic team, a new work often struggles, because it is built on inadequate or confused vision.

> Consequently, you are no longer foreigners and aliens, but fellow citizens with God's people and members of God's household, built on the foundation of the apostles and prophets, with Christ Jesus himself as the chief cornerstone. In him the whole building is joined together and rises to become a holy temple in the Lord. And in him you too are being built together to become a dwelling in which God lives by his Spirit (Eph 2:19-22).

The apostle and the prophet complement each other. So every church must be "built on the foundation of apostles and prophets". The apostle will use their pastoral experience to draw a group of believers together and build then into a unit. The prophet will impart vision and zeal into the new church, by encouraging the apostle and watching over the church to see that it is built according to God's plan.

Three important benefits come when a prophet and apostle work together.

- The prophet gives vision and direction.
- The prophet challenges the apostle if they take a wrong turn or go in the wrong direction.
- The prophet protects the people from the apostle.

Apostles can be dangerous. Most of the people around them have been blessed by them or discipled by them, so they tend to look up to the apostle. This means that an apostle is often surrounded by "Yes men", not because they are devious, but because they love and respect the apostle. An apostle needs someone bold enough to challenge them if they are mistaken. That task will usually fall to a prophet. Nathan took this role for David. Barnabas did it for Paul.

When a prophet colludes with the apostle to attack some of their people, life in the church gets dangerous. A prophet that starts firing the apostle's bullets becomes a pet prophet. This is a risk that all prophets should guard against.

## Travelling Prophets

When pastors are sent out to establish a beachhead in the enemy's territory, they become apostles. The church needs apostles and pastors.

- Pastors are local
- Apostles are mobile.

Apostles and pastors both need prophets alongside them. Pastors of local churches need prophets to feed holiness into their church. Apostles need prophets to ensure their new work is built on a solid foundation.

- Some prophets will be local, working with a pastor.
- Others will be mobile, working with an apostle.

There does not seem to be a role for independent mobile prophets. In the early church, groups of travelling prophets often lost the plot and became a burden on the church.

## No Prophetic Heroes
We must avoid the common error of making the ministry of the "prophet" too big. This happens when we model the prophetic ministry on the Old Testament. The problem is that these men were called to the role of Prophet to the Nation (described in the next chapter). To fulfil this calling they stood apart from the priests and kings. Only a few heroes had the necessary anointing of the Spirit.

The New Testament has not changed the role of the prophet, but it has changed the place where they function. A prophet is still a spokesperson for God, but the context in which they function has changed. Instead of standing apart, prophets should be an integral part of their church.

Since the coming of the Spirit, a person does not need to be an Elijah or Jeremiah to be a prophet or a spokesperson for God. In the same way a Christian does not need to be a Billy Graham to be an evangelist. A prophet is just an elder who fulfils the prophetic role in the leadership of the church.

In the Old Testament, the prophetic ministry was limited to a few heroes. With the coming of the Spirit, this calling will be much more widespread. Prophets should be everywhere. The intensity of their gifting may not always be as strong as Elijah or Jeremiah, but their prophetic ministry is just as valid. Every church should have a prophet.

## Personal Prophecy
Most prophets will begin by giving prophecies for individuals in their church. Personal prophecy is mostly for encouragement to build up their faith. The gift of prophecy is for strengthening, encouragement and comfort and to build up the body of Christ (1 Cor 14:3).

Personal prophecy will often be quite vague. However, Christians should not be living their lives in detailed obedience to the prophetic, so it does not matter if the words are fuzzy. We should be walking in obedience to the leading of the Holy Spirit and just getting confirmation, illumination or encouragement from personal prophecies. Therefore, these prophetic words do not need to be absolutely precise. Most personal prophecies convey a standard message.

- God is pleased with you.
- Keep on doing what you are doing.

God has a million ways of saying these words, but each one is perfect for the person who receives it. The important thing is that the word of prophecy is accompanied by the Holy Spirit moving in the heart of the hearer, so that the encouragement digs deep down into their soul and changes their attitude to life.

Some people are full of encouragement. They are great to be around. People with a pastoral calling should be bursting with encouragement, so they need to be fluent in the gift of prophecy. The irony is that regular anointing in the gift of prophecy may be a sign of a pastoral calling and not a sign of a prophetic calling.

Sometimes a warning will be needed. If a Christian is going the wrong way, they are unlikely to be turned round by the gift of prophecy. A warning is more likely received, if it comes from a trusted elder or friend with a prophetic gifting (Gal 6:1). David accepted correction from Nathan, because Nathan was his friend and a proven prophet (2 Sam 12).

## Prophecy to the Church

A problem occurs when a person who is fluent with the gift of prophecy and experienced with personal prophecy moves up to the role of bringing prophecy to a church. If a church is growing in obedience to the Holy Spirit, it will be filled with such a buzz that it does need much encouragement. If a church is wandering away from the true path, it will need correction. An example of this is the seven letters to the churches in Revelation 2,3.

I remember an incident when a prophetic word was spoken during the meeting of a church and all who were present fell on their knees and wept. We need to see more of this type of prophecy.

The problem is that most prophecies to churches are brought by pastors who are skilled in bringing encouragement to people through personal prophecy. These pastoral people carry over the same method and standard, so they proclaim encouragement to the church, but they struggle to bring a word of correction.

## Prophetic Excellence

The widespread acceptance of the prophetic ministry that emerged out of the Charismatic Renewal during the 1970s was a huge step forward for the church, but there is still a long way to go. An emphasis on quantity was okay while the gifting was re-emerging, but now that it is well established, we should be focussing more on quality.

Daniel and his mates did not just make a splash on Jewish bulletin boards, their insight and ability were recognised by a tough anti-god king.

> The king talked with them, and he found none equal to Daniel, Hananiah, Mishael and Azariah; so they entered the king's service. In every matter of wisdom and understanding about which the king questioned them, he found them ten times better than all the magicians and enchanters in his whole kingdom (Dan 1:19-20).

Daniel was recognised by worldly leaders as being ten times as wise as the other wise men of that time. That is why he got to serve three different kings in two world empires.

The Christian prophetic ministry should be aspiring to a similar level of excellence. Where are the Christian prophets who are recognised by the world as being ten times as discerning as other commentators? If we do not become complacent about the quality of prophecy, that level of gifting could emerge.

God has much more to give than we have seen so far. In the future, we will see much more tactical and strategic guidance coming from clear prophetic voices. The Old Testament prophets did not just predict calamities. They gave wise advise to local and national leaders (2 Chron 20:13-30). They also revealed God's long-term plans and strategy and what people should be doing to participate with God in work. Moses was a great prophet. He announced God's plan and timing for establishing people in the promised land. He also explained what Israel must do to enter into the land.

We have the fullness of the Holy Spirit, whereas in Old Testament times, the activity of the Holy Spirit was intermittent. Therefore, Christian prophets should be much more effective than the Old Testament prophets. We have a long way to go to achieve this. We must not be satisfied with what we have now, but press in to receive all that God has for us through the prophetic ministry.

## Men and Women

The ministry of the prophet is not limited to men. A woman can also be a prophet (prophetess).

> Even on my servants, both men and women, I will pour out my Spirit and they will prophesy (Acts 2:18).

Miriam was a prophetess (Num 12:6). So were the daughters of Philip the evangelist.

> He had four virgin daughters who were prophetesses (Acts 21:9).

Deborah and Anna were prophetesses.

> Deborah, a prophetess, the wife of Lappidoth, was leading Israel at that time. She held court under the Palm of Deborah…and the Israelites came to her to have their disputes decided (Jud 4:4-5).

> There was also a prophetess, Anna, the daughter of Phanuel, of the tribe of Asher. She was very old; she had lived with her husband seven years after her marriage, and then was a widow until she was eighty-four. She never left the temple but worshiped night and day, fasting and praying (Luke 2:36-37).

Prophetesses will sometimes function in a different way to male prophets, but most of the material in this book also applies to prophetesses.

## Calling

A true prophet must be called by God. The initiative in making a prophet always rests with him. It is not a ministry that anyone can choose. Only a false prophet dares to take up this ministry for himself. The true prophetic ministry always begins with a call from God. Isaiah had a very dramatic call (Isaiah 6:1-8). He needed this to sustain him through a difficult and disappointing ministry.

Jeremiah's calling came in a specific word from God when he was quite young.

> The word of the Lord came to me, saying, "Before I formed you in the womb I knew you, before you were born I set you apart; I appointed you as a prophet to the nations" (Jer 1:4-5).

Amos was going about his business when he received his call. He was not from a prophetic family and did not desire a prophetic ministry. Prophetic ambition is dangerous.

> Amos answered Amaziah, "I was neither a prophet nor a prophet's son, but I was a shepherd, and I also took care of sycamore-fig trees. But the Lord took me from tending the flock and said to me, 'Go, prophesy to my people Israel'" (Amos 7:14-15).

## Confirmation

Calling from God is essential for every Christian ministry. Acting without calling is presumption. Calling is particularly important for the prophetic ministry. The prophet who is not called is self-appointed, and self-appointed prophets are very dangerous.

The proof that a prophet has been called is words that are effective and fulfilled. Samuel is an example. All of Israel knew that he was a prophet, because the Lord was with him and let none of his words fall to the ground (1 Sam 3:19-20).

Calling comes from God, but it will also be confirmed and encouraged by other Christians. A calling that is not recognised by other Christians is often a deception and not a true calling.

*Only God can call a prophet. It is a sovereign choice of God. He can call anyone (Tom Marshall - The Coming of the Prophets).*

Young prophets should be careful about sharing the words of confirmation that the Lord has given about their calling. Most listeners will see this as boasting. They should only share these words with those who are close and who will understand them. The Lord gives these words to encourage the prophet, not to authenticate their ministry.

Prophetic people should avoid saying, "I am a Prophet", as it makes them sound arrogant. If you are a prophet, God will authenticate your ministry by fulfilling your words, as he did with Samuel. It is better to wait and let the people say, "He is a prophet", when they see your words confirmed and fulfilled by the Holy Spirit.

Calling is confirmed by preparation. There is often a long gap between the time of God's calling and entry into ministry. This calls for patience. Preparation may take a lot longer than we expect, but God's standards are high.

*After every calling and envisioning comes a time of death and burial. It is called preparation, as the Lord puts our call on the shelf and deals with who we are as people. During this "in the ground" time, the reality of the call leaves us for a time. Therefore, when suddenly someone begins to restate our call prophetically, it may be the time when the Lord is opening doors and making things happen (Graeme Cooke - Developing your Prophetic Ministry).*

## Wife of a Prophet

Some prophets will be single, but many will be married. The wife of a prophet often carries a heavy burden.

Men called to the prophetic ministry are usually very thick skinned. They need to be to fulfil their calling.

> I will make you as unyielding and hardened as they are. I will make your forehead like the hardest stone, harder than flint (Ez 3:8-9).

> Today I have made you a fortified city, an iron pillar and a bronze wall to stand against the whole land-the kings of Judah, its officials its priests and the people (Jer 1:18).

The wife of the prophet is not a fortified city. She is a precious vessel (1 Peter 3:7), who is vulnerable to attack. Because opposites attract, she can often be a very sensitive person.

As a prophet moves into his calling, he must put protection in place for his wife. She needs to be surrounded by loyal and sympathetic friends, who understand her struggle and can provide encouragement and support. His calling to be a prophet must not be put ahead of his responsibility to nurture and protect his wife. She must not be sacrificed on the altar of the prophetic ministry.

When he receives a hard word, the prophet will have wrestled with God and gone through a process to be sure that the word is correct. His wife has not gone through that process, so she will not be so sure that the word is right. She will remember the times when her husband has been wrong, whereas he will have pushed these down into a memory hole, so he can get on with his ministry. She will remember the harm done, and be concerned that he could be wrong again, so it will be difficult for her to share the same confidence in his words. He should acknowledge her fear and help her to understand why he believes the word is true. She will need to trust him, for better or for worse.

People are often intimidated by a prophet. If they disagree with what he has spoken, they will often be scared to challenge him. Many will take the easy way out, and share their concerns with his wife, hoping that she will pass them on to her husband. This is a bad practice. The wife should point out that her husband is teachable and encourage the people to take their concerns to him directly. The elders should advise the people in the church not to mess with his wife, if they have an issue with the prophet.

Prophets tend to be very black and white, so they can easily hurt people. When a young prophet is starting out, he will not even be aware that he is doing this. The prophet's wife will be much more sensitive to what is happening. She will notice all the unnecessary hurt and pain that he has caused. The prophet should learn from his wife by asking how people respond to the way he speaks. He should use her advice to learn to speak the truth in love. Being a prophet is a tough calling. The wife of a prophet knows his integrity and the cost of his ministry, so she can be his main source of encouragement.

The experience will be different for husbands of prophetesses. Their main challenge will be to ensure that their wives are not overworked by the church. They will need to check that Christians are not taking advantage of their wife's good nature, when they should be seeking God for themselves. When a prophetess is attacked, her husband should stand beside her to protect her from abuse.

## Prophetic Teams

When several prophets function together, the anointing is multiplied, not added. The Holy Spirit loves to chop a revelation up like a jigsaw and give pieces to different people and then watch their excitement as they put it back together.

The other side is that lone prophets can often assume that they have the whole picture when they have only received part of it. The piece of the jigsaw that they hold might be pretty, but they will need to get together with others to see the full picture. Partial messages given by lone prophets are a serious problem for the church.

The one-one man band was never part of God's economy. The lone prophet (and the lone evangelist, and the lone pastor) should never have got past Pentecost. The big man syndrome is a curse on the church. God's way is a big Holy Spirit working through a whole lot of little people.

The best antidote to heroic prophets is a prophetic community. The full revelation of God will be received by a group of people seeking him together. The Holy Spirit will give different parts of the revelation to different people. The full picture will be obtained by pooling all the information.

*God is wanting to raise up prophetic communities. Individual prophets are not capable of hearing Gods word for our complex world (Tom Marshall - The Coming of the Prophets).*

While there is strength in several prophets working together (1 Cor 14:29) there are also risks. A group of prophets working together can rark each other up in the flesh. The result is not a pretty sight. Miciah faced a situation where this had happened (1 Kings 22:12-13).

When prophets get together, God prefers that someone with a pastoral gifting is present as well. They will help the prophets to keep their feet on the ground. Balanced ministry provides real safety.

## Urgent

The most urgent need in the church today, is the restoration of the prophetic ministry. Prophets are absolutely essential for the operation of the church. God cannot complete his work until the prophetic ministry is restored. God promised that he would never leave his people without prophets who could speak his word. In Deuteronomy 18:18, God promises his people that he will always provide them with a prophet who will speak his word.

> I will raise up for them a prophet like you (Moses) from among their brothers. I will put my words in his mouth, and he will tell them everything that I command him.

This promise had an ultimate fulfilment in Jesus, but it is also a promise that we should claim for our time.

> *The task of the prophetic imagination is to bring to public expression those very hopes and yearnings that have been denied so long and suppressed so deeply that we no longer know they are there (Walter Brueggemann - The Prophetic Imagination).*

# 2

# Character of a Prophet

A prophet is God's spokesperson on earth. Speaking for God is impossible unless some of the character of God is manifested. Godly character is essential.

*God is more concerned that we embody the message than that we preserve our reputation (Mike Bickle - Growing in the Prophetic).*

Some of the key virtues that will be present in a prophet are as follows.

## a) Power of the Spirit

Prophets must be full of the power of the Holy Spirit. Without the Holy Spirit, a prophet cannot function and will be just a babbling voice. The scriptures are clear that prophets must have the Spirit of God upon them.

> By your Spirit you admonished them through your prophets (Neh 9:30).

> I wish that all the Lord's people were prophets and that the Lord would put his spirit on them (Num 11:29).

> I will pour out my Spirit on all people your sons and your daughters will prophesy (Acts 2:17).

*The prophet should be careful to walk in the Spirit all the time. He is to pray constantly. This often means silent prayer in tongues (John and Paula Sanford - The Elijah Task).*

## b) Total Obedience

A prophet must be totally obedient to God. The prophetic ministry requires a higher standard of holiness than other ministries. 1 Kings 13 tells of a young prophet, who started well, but ended in disaster, because he failed to obey the word that God had spoken to him. All prophets should read this passage frequently.

> This is what the Lord says: "You have defied the word of the Lord and have not kept the command the Lord your God gave you. You came back, ate bread, and drank water in the place where he told you not to eat or drink. Therefore your body will not be buried in the tomb of your fathers." When the man of God had finished eating and drinking, the prophet who had brought him back saddled his donkey for him. As he went on his way, a lion met him on the road and killed him, and his body was thrown down on the road, with both the donkey and the lion standing beside it. Some people who passed by saw the body thrown down there, with the lion standing beside the body, and they went and reported it in the city (1 Kings 13:21-25).

Balaam did not practice what he preached, but he was very aware of the importance of obedience to God.

> But can I say just anything? I must speak only what God puts in my mouth (Num 22:38).

Elisha became a prophet by forsaking his life as a farmer and becoming an attendant to Elijah. He learned obedience by serving an older prophet.

> So Elisha left him and went back. Then he set out to follow Elijah and became his attendant (1 Kings 19:21).

*There must be radical pursuit of Jesus to get the pure word of the Lord. Mature prophets are so in love with Jesus and submitted to His Lordship, that they are willing to see the word come back into His hand after receiving it. They won't care whether it is used or simply poured out on the ground (not used) as an offering to the Lord. Words received and given from such a heart of obedience give more life and blessing than those presumptuously spoken (Steve Shultz - Elijah List).*

30

## c) Peace with God

The prophetic person must be at peace with God. They must always speak out of their relationship with God and not out of reaction to a situation.

> *Prophetic ministry requires a profound communion with God (Ian Breward).*

When a prophet gets it wrong, the solution is to repent and turn back to the Lord. A prophet must keep a short slate with the Lord. God promised protection to Jeremiah, while he had a repentant attitude.

> If you repent, I will restore you that you may serve me; if you utter worthy, not worthless, words, you will be my spokesman. Let this people turn to you, but you must not turn to them. I will make you a wall to this people, a fortified wall of bronze; they will fight against you but will not overcome you, for I am with you to rescue and save you (Jer 15:19-20).

## d) Patience

Waiting is an important aspect of the prophetic ministry. Much time will be spent waiting on God. Even more time will be spent waiting for his word to be fulfilled. Those who are impatient will become very frustrated. Patience comes out of a dedicated commitment to God and his purposes.

The Bible confirms that the time between a word being spoken and its fulfilment can be quite long.

> He replied, "Go your way, Daniel, because the words are closed up and sealed until the time of the end" (Dan 12:9).

*Visionary faith takes on itself the crushing weight of the contradictions of reality. It is often just before the breakthrough that pressure is most intense and faith seems to shudder under the strain. This strain is what causes doubt. The immense weight of contradictory reality crashes against faith. This is not easy. It is one thing to be fired by a vision and get out of an armchair. It is another thing to be fired by a vision and walk through fire and rain (Os Guiness).*

31

*Between every vision and its fulfilment is an arduous path. So if all hell seems to have broken loose and nothing is going right, rejoice and praise God under your sufferings. The afflictions may confirm your vision more than anything else. God is breaking you in order that the fulfilment of the vision may be of him (John Sanford).*

*Part of the problem associated with prophets arises because they often see things that others don't. And they usually see them long before they come to pass. This can be a frustrating position to be in (Tom Hamon - The Spirit of Wisdom and Revelation).*

## e) Boldness and Sensitivity

A prophet needs enormous boldness to speak God's truth to hostile and powerful people. A prophet also needs enormous sensitivity, to hear Gods heart and demonstrate his love. There are plenty of bold people who wade in boots and all, and plenty of sensitive people who would not say boo to a mouse, but only a rare few can combine the boldness and the sensitivity needed to be a prophet to the nation. Jeremiah demonstrated both.

## f) Integrity and honesty

The first loyalty of a prophet is to the truth. For prophets to have credibility, truth must permeate their entire being.

*But Elijah was fierce and ruthless when he came to issues of truth. There will never be glory in the church till this spirit is restored. It is contrary to the spirit of the age: compromise. God is fierce and jealous for truth. He hates sin, inequity unrighteousness and compromise (Art Katz - The Heart of a Prophet).*

## g) Humility

Pride kills prophets. Vanity is a terrible threat to prophetic ministry. God will have to establish a deep work of humility in the life of anyone he intends to speak for him.

*Refuse to promote yourself, "your" word, or "your" ministry. If God gives you something to say, let Him see to the promotion of it (Chip Brogden - Letter to a Reluctant Prophet).*

*No one will graduate from the Lord's school of listening with his pride intact. In fact no one will ever really become adept in the art of listening. There are simply those who know that God can speak to them and who plead that His mercy may continually override their stubborn hearts and minds. We must remain fumbling children starting from ground zero, to hear God anew every day (John and Paula Sanford - The Elijah Task).*

*Another trap into which I commonly see prophetic people fall is the desire to be awesome in ministry, to be "a prophet to the nations". This is exactly the opposite of the true spirit of prophecy… Prophecy is meant to testify to the awesomeness of Jesus not to the prophetic ministry (Jack Deere - Surprised by the Voice of God).*

## h) Compassion

Old Testament prophets are often portrayed as harsh, uncompromising men. This is incorrect: They were uncompromising but they were never harsh. They shed more tears than priests and kings, because compassion was at the heart of their ministry. God is love, so his truth must always be spoken in love. The harder the message the prophet is speaking, the more important that it is spoken with compassion. Jeremiah wept over the words he spoke.

> Since my people are crushed, I am crushed; I mourn, and horror grips me. Is there no balm in Gilead? Is there no physician there? Why then is there no healing for the wound of my people? Oh, that my head were a spring of water and my eyes a fountain of tears! I would weep day and night for the slain of my people (Jer 8:21-9:1).

*There is a deep compassion running right through the ministry of the prophets that reveals their understanding of God as merciful, compassionate and over flowing with loving kindness (Clifford Hill).*

*The cry from God's heart comes from a man with tear stained face and a sob in his throat. He felt as few have ever felt, the brokenness of God's heart for Israel, God's beloved people. It was only through the deep waters of suffering, that he could understand and appreciate something of the wounded love of God (Milton Smith- Hosea).*

### i) Tenacity and commitment

All prophets will meet with opposition. Jeremiah is an example of a prophet who was treated cruelly.

> Shephatiah son of Mattan, Gedaliah son of Pashhur, Jehucal son of Shelemiah, and Pashhur son of Malkijah heard what Jeremiah was telling all the people... So they took Jeremiah and put him into the cistern of Malkijah, the king's son, which was in the courtyard of the guard. They lowered Jeremiah by ropes into the cistern; it had no water in it, only mud, and Jeremiah sank down into the mud (Jer 38:1-6).

Sometimes the most intense opposition comes from the people who know the prophet well. Jeremiah was warned not to trust his own family.

> If you have raced with men on foot and they have worn you out, how can you compete with horses? If you stumble in safe country, how will you manage in the thickets by the Jordan? Your brothers, your own family even they have betrayed you; they have raised a loud cry against you. Do not trust them, though they speak well of you (Jer 12:5-6).

Jesus warned that a prophet has no honour in their own country (John 4:44). Prophets must meet opposition with tenacity and commitment to God's purpose. Once called, a prophet must be steadfast in their ministry. They cannot swerve to the left or the right. Their loyalty to God must never be shaken, whatever the circumstances.

> *All the prophets encounter opposition, but one of the marks of the true prophet was fortitude with which he met the opposition and the tenacity with which he continued to proclaim the message. Each of the prophets displayed the quality of total commitment to the ministry to which he was called. There was no turning back or weakening. Once the prophet had embarked upon his public ministry, he was marked out as a man of God. His loyalty was to God alone whatever the consequences. Each of the prophets was driven by a kind of inner compulsion to fulfil whatever task was given regardless of the danger of or personal suffering that may result (Clifford Hill - Prophecy, Past and Present).*

Prophets are often so task-focused that they suffer from a compulsion to fulfil their calling, no matter what it will cost them. Jeremiah understood that he must not let anything stop him from fulfilling his calling.

> O Lord, you deceived me, and I was deceived; you overpowered me and prevailed. I am ridiculed all day long; everyone mocks me. Whenever I speak, I cry out proclaiming violence and destruction. So the word of the Lord has brought me insult and reproach all day long. But if I say, "I will not mention him or speak any more in his name," his word is in my heart like a fire, a fire shut up in my bones. I am weary of holding it in; indeed, I cannot. I hear many whispering, "Terror on every side! Report him! Let's report him!" All my friends are waiting for me to slip, saying, "Perhaps he will be deceived; then we will prevail over him and take our revenge on him (Jer 20:7-10).

*Jeremiah appears to be a pessimist. There were times of very deep depression when he seems to have laboured in vain and to have spent his strength for nought; so that he almost resolved to speak no more in the name of the Lord. But Jeremiah had misunderstood God's promise; which was not that God would deliver him out of his suffering, but that he would keep him in his suffering (Milton Smith).*

God warned Ezekiel that he would need tenacity in the face of opposition.

> He said to me, "Son of man, stand up on your feet and I will speak to you." As he spoke, the Spirit came into me and raised me to my feet, and I heard him speaking to me. He said: "Son of man, I am sending you to the Israelites, to a rebellious nation that has rebelled against me; they and their fathers have been in revolt against me to this very day. The people to whom I am sending you are obstinate and stubborn. Say to them, 'This is what the Sovereign Lord says.' And whether they listen or fail to listen-for they are a rebellious house-they will know that a prophet has been among them. And you, son of man, do not be afraid of them or their words. Do not be afraid, though briars and thorns are all around you and you live among scorpions. Do not be afraid of what they say or terrified

by them, though they are a rebellious house. You must speak my words to them, whether they listen or fail to listen, for they are rebellious" (Ezek 2:1-7).

*He is fanatical! It is not just to announce the purpose, but to demand that everything else be related to it. That is prophetic intensity and prophetic insistence. We are not only to understand the ultimate and full purposes of God, but everything else that constitutes our life and being is to be related to that. That will require a radical adjustment, and that is why prophets are not popular. That requirement is painful and that is why people do not want to hear it (Art Katz – What is the Prophetic Church).*

## j) Boldness and courage

Loyalty to God will manifest in courage and boldness. There are numerous examples of prophets standing boldly in the face of political powers. They were often in danger of losing their lives. The Lord told Ezekiel as part of his call that he would need great boldness.

> He then said to me: "Son of man, go now to the house of Israel and speak my words to them. You are not being sent to a people of obscure speech and difficult language, but to the house of Israel—not to many peoples of obscure speech and difficult language, whose words you cannot understand. Surely if I had sent you to them, they would have listened to you. But the house of Israel is not willing to listen to you because they are not willing to listen to me, for the whole house of Israel is hardened and obstinate. But I will make you as unyielding and hardened as they are. I will make your forehead like the hardest stone, harder than flint. Do not be afraid of them or terrified by them, though they are a rebellious house." And he said to me, "Son of man, listen carefully and take to heart all the words I speak to you" (Ezek 3:4-10).

Fulfilling the prophetic ministry will take great mental and spiritual toughness. This is doubly true, when the church is weak or rebellious and disinterested in the prophetic voice.

*Expect misunderstanding. Expect persecution. Expect ridicule. Expect mistreatment. Expect suffering. Expect rejection. Then, you won't be surprised when it comes (Chip Brogden - Letter to a Reluctant Prophet).*

During times of rebellion against God, prophets will be rejected and misunderstood.

> Because your sins are so many and your hostility so great, the prophet is considered a fool, the inspired person a maniac (Hos 9:7).

God has promised that he will protect those who serve and obey him. The following passages are just a few examples.

> As the enemy came down toward him, Elisha prayed to the Lord, "Strike these people with blindness." So he struck them with blindness, as Elisha had asked (2 Kings 6:18).

> When they were but few in number, few indeed, and strangers in it, they wandered from nation to nation, from one kingdom to another. He allowed no man to oppress them; for their sake he rebuked kings: "Do not touch my anointed ones; do my prophets no harm" (1 Chron 16:19-22; Ps 105:12-15).

## Prophets are Different

Prophets do not fit in easily and often seem to be misfits. They often seem to be off on a tangent, worrying about something that most people do not care about. The prophet is often out of step with the mood of the times.

> *The Christian prophets' power is to humble the mighty and to raise the destitute. When others are laughing, he weeps in spirit, and when they weep, spirit rejoices. For he is one step ahead in vision, and in the burden on spirit. The Lord is the forerunner, but he is most often that forerunner through his prophets. They go before him to prepare his way in the body. When the church is rejoicing and celebrating the victory of the Lord, the prophet is already called to the next battle, the next pit of sorrow. The next work of the Lord is upon him. When the body of Christ is grovelling in pain and repentance, the prophet is rejoicing both that the body is repenting and that the reward of the Lord's mercy is coming.*

> *To a person endowed with prophetic insight, everyone else appears blind; to a person whose ear perceives God's voice, everyone else appears deaf. No one is just; no knowing is strong enough, no trust complete enough. The prophet hates the approximate, he shuns the middle of the road. Man must live on the summit to avoid the abyss. There is nothing to hold to*

*except God. Carried away by the challenge, the demand to straighten out man's ways, the prophet is strange, one-sided, an unbearable extremist. The prophet disdains those for who God's presence is comfort and security; to him it is a challenge, an incessant demand. God is compassion, not compromise; justice, though not inclemency. The prophet's predictions can always be proved wrong by a change in man's conduct, but never the certainty that God is full of compassion. The prophet's word is a scream in the night. While the world is at ease and asleep, the prophet feels the blast from heaven (Abraham Heschel - The Prophets).*

*Prophets are not interested in consequences only in God's will. There is a divine madness that marks the Old Testament prophets. This is uncomfortable to have beside the way we operate (Ian Breward).*

Be careful! Being different does not make you a prophet. The same symptoms are present in people who are rebellious or have a bad attitude. Many difficult and contentious Christians think they are being prophetic, when they are really just being a nuisance, because they have sin issues that they have refused to deal with. They give the prophetic ministry a bad name.

## Preparation

This high standard of character does not come easily. God will spend many years preparing his prophets, generally by putting them "through the mill".

*What discipline, training and chastisement is required! The prophet, more than all others, save the apostle, must die to self, daily. His word must not be his own. What dire warnings Jeremiah 23 and Ezekiel 13 heap upon the soulish prophet who speaks not out of God's Spirit but from the contrary winds of his own soul. No beginner can be that pure. God teaches in the rude world of trial and error. Therefore the budding prophet will be thrashed, beaten, humiliated, scorned, laughed at, and rejected, will fall into error and arise—only to fall again, until, in every part of him, like Nebuchadnezzar, he knows—with grass in mouth that the "Most High rules the kingdom of men and gives it to whom he will" (John and Paula Sanford - The Elijah Task).*

*Sometimes the preparation of the prophet may include a period of isolation in the wilderness. Moses spent forty years in the wilderness watching sheep, while God prepared him for his calling (T. Austin-Sparks - What is Prophetic Ultimacy).*

Preparation and character development often come through suffering. This is especially true for those called to a higher level of prophetic ministry. Great intensity of preparation and holiness will be required. This is particularly important in times of apostasy and rebellion against God. Troubled times call for drastic and radical ministry. However, for most people, being prophetic will be much simpler. They will be the member of the eldership team who asks the hard questions and challenges sin in all its forms. They may not need the same intensity of preparation, but they will still need to manifest all the characteristics outlined above.

*God is more concerned with the messenger than the message. Do you see that the minister is more important than the ministry? If the messenger is wrong, the message will be wrong too. If the minister is wrong, the ministry will be wrong. And do you see that the Lord of the work is more important than the work of the Lord? Meditate on these things (Chip Brogden - Letter to a Reluctant Prophet).*

*In the long run no man can have high visions and lead a low life (TC Gordon).*

*Prophets should be sons of Issachar, men who understand the time; they must not be sons of thunder, who do not know what they are doing.*

# 3
# Role of a Prophet

A prophet is a spokesperson for God. They admonish, warn, direct, encourage, intercede, teach and counsel. They bring the word of God to the people of God and call the people to respond.

Prophetic ministry begins in the presence of the Lord. This aspect of the ministry is well described in Jeremiah's challenge to the false prophets.

> Which of them has stood in the council of the Lord to see or to hear his word? If they had stood in his council they would have proclaimed his words to people and they would have turned from their evil ways and from their evil deeds (Jer 23:18,22).

The prophet stands before the people as one who has stood before God. They know the heart and mind of the Lord, so they can speak the word of the Lord to his people. Because their words come from the heart of God, they are powerful and effective.

A prophet can undertake a huge variety of roles. This is an expression of the creativity of God. No two prophets will be the same, but each will be a reflection of God's creativity and calling.

## a) Prayer

Prayer is an important part of the prophetic task. Because prophets know the mind of the Lord, they are in a position to pray effectively. They have a clear picture of what God is doing, so they know where prayer is needed most. Prophets watch over the word of the Lord and pray it into being. They cannot rest until God's word is fulfilled (Isaiah 62:6).

*An important part of the prophet's task is unceasing prayer for the Christian Community. The prophets, because they knew what the mind of the Lord was, were in a position to pray more effectually than other men. They had a clearer picture of what God was doing and so they knew when prayer was needed most. They were also able to pray true 'prophetic prayers' in which the Holy Spirit directed and guided their very manner and words (Bruce Yocum - Prophecy and Prayer).*

*Prayer belongs in a very high and important sense to the prophetic ministry. Praying prophets have frequently been at a premium in the history of God's people. God's watchmen must always and everywhere be men of prayer. Praying preachers are the true prophets of the Lord, and are they who stand as mouth pieces of God to a generation of wicked and worldly-minded men and women. They are the boldest and truest, and swiftest ministers of God (E.M Bounds - The Weapon of Prayer).*

## b) Receiving the Word of the Lord

A key role of the prophet is waiting in the presence of the Spirit to receive the word of God. God is sovereign so we cannot tell him when he should speak. Hearing will usually require waiting, and more waiting.

*The task of the prophets was to know the will of God, so that they could convey it to the nation. Their ministry consisted in handling revelation, ie the knowledge that God has revealed to them. From the earliest times prophecy was conceived as being the activity of God, rather than the activity of man. This is true not only for the receiving of prophecy but also for it's delivery. When the prophecy actually conveyed the word of the Lord to the people he was deemed to be under the power of God. The hand of the Lord was upon him, empowering and directing the delivery of the word (Clifford Hill - Prophecy, Past and Present).*

## c) Suffering

A prophet is often called to suffering. Deep dealing by the hand of God will often be needed to prepare the prophets for receiving the word of God. Sometimes they may actually have to experience beforehand, something of what their people will experience. Jeremiah spent many years in captivity before his people went into captivity. He was often rejected and ostracised; he was even accused of being a traitor. Ezekiel had to lie on his side for 390 days to symbolise the judgement that would come upon his nation. This suffering made the prophets extremely aware of their human frailty (Jer 20:7-10). It also equipped them to give a very harsh message in a spirit of compassion.

A true message is nullified if it is spoken in the wrong spirit. Suffering softens the prophet's spirit, so a hard word can be given in a spirit of love. Suffering contributed to Jeremiah's compassion.

> When the priest Pashhur son of Immer, the chief officer in the temple of the Lord, heard Jeremiah prophesying these things, he had Jeremiah the prophet beaten and put in the stocks at the Upper Gate of Benjamin at the Lord's temple (Jer 20:1-2).

In the faith chapter of Hebrews, several prophets are recorded as heroes who suffered for their calling.

> And what more shall I say? I do not have time to tell about Gideon, Barak, Samson, Jephthah, David, Samuel and the prophets, who through faith conquered kingdoms, administered justice, and gained what was promised; Others were tortured and refused to be released, so that they might gain a better resurrection. Some faced jeers and flogging, while still others were chained and put in prison. They were stoned; they were sawed in two; they were put to death by the sword. They went about in sheepskins and goatskins, destitute, persecuted and mistreated-- the world was not worthy of them. They wandered in deserts and mountains, and in caves and holes in the ground (Heb 11:32-38).

*There is an especial message in the ministry of Jeremiah for those who are compelled to stand alone, who fall into the ground to die, who fill up what is behind of the sufferings of Christ, and through death arise to bear fruit in the great world of men, which they passionately love (F.B Meyer - Jeremiah).*

*A prophetic ministry involves having a foretaste of the suffering and judgement that will come as a result of the sins of the church and the whole world, since iniquity would soon be universal. In such a commission one must be willing to pay the price involved in foreseeing the coming events, in suffering and experiencing them in advance. Only then can the warning be passed on (A W Pink).*

*Confrontation is right at the centre of the prophetic calling. A prophet is one in whom the Lord has invested a lifetime of preparation for one final hour of confrontation (Art Katz - The Heart of a Prophet).*

## d) Encouragement

Encouragement of other Christians is an important aspect of the prophetic ministry.

> Everyone who prophesies speaks to men for their strengthening, encouragement and comfort... he who prophesies edifies the church (1 Cor 14:3-4).

The words of the prophets will build up and strengthen the church. This will be especially important in times of trial and tribulation. Silas and Judas were prophets who encouraged the church in Antioch.

> Judas and Silas, who themselves were prophets, said much to encourage and strengthen the brothers (Acts 15:32).

The scriptures give a number of examples of prophets who encouraged the leaders of their nation to act boldly.

> When Asa heard these words and the prophecy of Azariah son of Oded the prophet, he took courage (2 Chron 15:8).

> Then Haggai, the Lord's messenger, gave this message of the Lord to the people: "I am with you," declares the Lord. So the Lord stirred up the spirit of Zerubbabel son of Shealtiel, governor of Judah, and the spirit of Joshua son of Jehozadak, the high priest, and the spirit of the whole remnant of the people (Hag 1:13-14).

## e) Worship

The prophetic ministry can often play an important part in worship. Paul said that when the church gathered together,

> Two or three prophets should speak, and the others should weigh carefully what is said. And if a revelation comes to someone who is sitting down, the first speaker should stop. For you can all prophesy in turn so that everyone may be instructed and encouraged. The spirits of prophets are subject to the control of prophets. For God is not a God of disorder but of peace (1 Cor 14:29-33).

A prophecy that speaks of the glory and wonder of God will inspire his people to worship. Miriam, the prophetess led the children of Israel in worship after they had crossed the Red Sea (Exodus 15:19-21). 1 Chronicles 25 lists a number of people who were set aside for the ministry of prophesying to the accompaniment of musical instruments as part of the temple worship. They were professional worshippers and prophets, responsible for leading the worship in the house of God. This ministry is needed today. In small fellowships, it can be provided by the gift of prophecy. Large meetings for celebration will benefit from prophets who can bring a word from the Lord to build the worship.

> David, together with the commanders of the army, set apart some of the sons of Asaph, Heman and Jeduthun for the ***ministry of prophesying, accompanied by harps***, lyres and cymbals. Here is the list of the men who performed this service: ....... All these men were under the supervision of their fathers for the music of the temple of the Lord, with cymbals, lyres and harps, for the ministry at the house of God. Asaph, Jeduthun and Heman were under the supervision of the king. Along with their relatives all of them trained and skilled in music for the Lord they numbered 288 (1 Chron 25:1,6-7).

## f) Foretelling the Future

Prediction of the future is part of the prophetic ministry. Almost every prophet in the Old Testament appeared first as a foreteller. Through their fellowship with the eternal God, the prophets have access to the future. They are seers who have insight into God's purposes for history. However, what they see for the future is always connected to the present. They warn of future judgements so that people will change their behaviour now. They speak of future blessing to give hope in the present.

Prophets speak to the present, in light of the future that God has revealed. For example, Isaiah warned Hezekiah to put his house in order because he would die soon.

> In those days, Hezekiah became ill and was at the point of death. The prophet Isaiah son of Amoz went to him and said, "This is what the Lord says: Put your house in order, because you are going to die; you will not recover." Hezekiah turned his face to the wall and prayed to the Lord (2 Kings 20:1-2).

> *Calls to repentance and calls to practical holiness are based on a word concerning the future; the vision of wrath to come is the basis of a present seeking of the mercy of God (J.A Motyer - New Bible Dictionary).*

## g) Direction and Guidance

Prophets bring the word of the Lord to the church. Christians can be so caught up in the events of the world that they do not see what God is doing. This is particularly true in tumultuous times, when it can be very hard to see the hand of God at work. Prophets will give direction and vision in these situations, so that God's people know what is happening, and what they should do. For example, the prophet Gad provided guidance to David and showed him how to avoid trouble.

> But the prophet Gad said to David, "Do not stay in the stronghold. Go into the land of Judah." So David left and went to the forest of Hereth (1 Sam 22:5).

Prophets can give direction to those who are seeking the will of God. Sometimes the prophetic word will be for the church as a whole, or for the leadership of the church.

*Prophets must know God and understand the world and bring God's revelation to bear on it to show people where it is going. They should show people what to do next (Ian Breward).*

Personal prophecy must be treated with caution. The gift of prophecy is not usually directive, so it is dangerous to make life-changing decisions on the basis of a prophecy uttered by a person who has not been recognised as a prophet.

Prophets will sometimes give direction, but generally this should come as a confirmation of something that God has already spoken to the person concerned. God wants to lead his people by his Spirit. He wants every believer to learn how to hear the Spirit's voice. A message from a prophet should normally come as a confirmation of something that the Spirit has already spoken.

Getting confirmation from a prophet before we act can be really encouraging, but we need to be very careful. A personal prophecy can be misleading if we have let our own plans and desires control our thinking. Ezekiel gives a surprising warning.

> When any of the Israelites set up idols in their hearts and put a wicked stumbling block before their faces and then go to a prophet, I the Lord will answer them myself in keeping with their great idolatry (Ezek 14:4).

If a person has let something that they want become an idol in their heart, God may prophesy to them what they want to hear. If the person acts on the prophecy, it will lead to disaster. God does this to reveal the idol and recapture the person's heart. If a prophecy confirms what we want to do, it may just be a sign that we have made our own plans into an "idol in the heart".

Making decisions on the basis of a word from another person is dangerous. It is wrong to be totally dependent on others for guidance. Many Christians have been led astray because they did get their own word from God.

> *Christian prophets do not tell people what to do, they confirm what God is saying. To go to a Christian prophet for direction and guidance is to violate the New Covenant which gives us direct access and approach to God through Christ by the Spirit (Graham Cooke - Developing Your Prophetic Gifting).*
>
> *Telling the people what they want to hear at the expense of what they need to hear weakens the church. It causes people to seek the gifts and manifestations to the neglect of pursuing the character of God (John Bevere - Thus Saith the Lord).*

## h) Interpreting Dreams and Visions

An important aspect of the prophetic ministry is interpreting dreams and visions. God often speaks in dreams to break into people who are not listening. We must learn to interpret their meaning to understand what he is saying. Prophets are sometimes skilled in interpreting dreams. Daniel was a prophet who was skilled with dreams (Daniel 2:1-28).

> During the night the mystery was revealed to Daniel in a vision. Then Daniel praised the God of heaven and said: "Praise be to the name of God for ever and ever; wisdom and power are his. He changes times and seasons; he sets up kings and deposes them. He gives wisdom to the wise and knowledge to the discerning. He reveals deep and hidden things; he knows what lies in darkness, and light dwells with him. I thank and praise you, O God of my fathers: you have given me wisdom and power, you have made known to me what we asked of you, you have made known to us the dream of the king" (Dan 2:19-23).

Dreams often include people and objects with which we are familiar used in symbolic ways. We must not assume that they will be fulfilled literally. For example, Joseph saw the sun, moon and eleven stars bowing before him. This was not literally fulfilled, but he eventually saw his father and eleven brothers bowing before him (Genesis 37:5-10; 40:5-22; 44:14).

Dreams should be interpreted like parables. Kings and rulers will often hear God through dreams. Prophets can help them to understand what God is saying.

> It is the glory of God to conceal a matter; to search out a matter is the glory of Kings (Prov 25:2).

## i) Correction and Admonition

There is also a negative side to the ministry of the prophet. This can be seen in the calling of Jeremiah:

> See, today I appoint you over nations and kingdoms to uproot and tear down, to destroy and overthrow to build and to plant (Jer 1:10).

Four of the six expressions used by God to describe Jeremiah's ministry are negative. God sometimes has to uproot and tear down, destroy and overthrow, before he can begin to plant and build. Prophets co-operate with God in breaking down all that is not built on the true foundation. They do this by announcing his judgements. At the same time, they watch over all that God is building to see that it is built according to his Word. This is an important task, because God cannot complete his restoration work until the prophetic ministry is restored.

> *Two thirds of his work was therefore in the direction of destruction. It is not pleasant or easy work (F.B Meyer - Jeremiah).*

> *It was Jeremiah's lot to prophesy at a time when all things in Judah were running down in a final and mournful catastrophe, when political excitement was at its height and the most fatal counsels prevailed. It was his role to stand in the way, over which his nation was pushing headlong to destruction: to make an heroic effort to arrest it and to turn it back; and to fail his and be compelled to step to one side and see his own people, whom he loved with the tenderness of a woman plunge over the precipice into the wide weltering ruin (Dr Moorehead).*

> *The prophetic voice of Israel was primarily a word of judgement upon the people of God. So the prophetic voice of the church must be a word which warns of impending judgement upon the church. Warning to the world is secondary (Os Guiness).*

Paul described a prophetic ministry that cut to the hearts of the people.

> But if an unbeliever or someone who does not understand comes in while everybody is prophesying, he will be convinced by all that he is a sinner and will be judged by all, and the secrets of his heart will be laid bare. So he will fall down and worship God, exclaiming, "God is really among you!" (1 Cor 14:24-25).

*The prophet's job is lonely. He is usually a one-man verbal demolition team. He must attack the root of the evil, which goes very deep and affects everything. He does not criticise this or that evil; he criticises the system that produced a forest of bad trees and bad fruit. He is not a tree-trimmer; he is in the tree-uprooting business (Gary North - Prophets, Leaders, Followers, Losers).*

Amos was a prophet who understood the condition of his nation, and knew the issues in Israel with which God took exception. It is not the worldly society, but God's people with whom God is primarily concerned and with whom he will first enter into judgement.

Elijah was a confrontation prophet. God used him to confront the evils of his time.

## j) Exposing Rotten Leadership

Rotten leadership has done terrible damage in the church, by imparting sin and evil spirits to hundreds and thousands of ordinary people who trusted their leaders and were vulnerable because they submitted to them. When the leadership of a church is rotten, the prophet must expose it.

The reality is that a prophet is not needed to expose most problems within church leadership. The people who are close to their leader usually know what is going on. The problem is that they are too loyal to challenge the leader that they look up to. The prophet is usually the only one tough enough to call the leader on their faults.

God has provided a way to protect leaders and people, but the church consistently refuses to adopt it. Leadership incidents will only stop when the church goes back to balanced ministry, with churches led by a team of pastors, prophets and evangelists working together in submission to each other. As long as we perpetuate the myth that one guy must be top dog, embarrassing incidents will continue to shame the church and hurt innocent Christians. God cannot protect his people from evil, while the leaders of his church refuse to adopt the spiritual protection he has provided. Prophets should be exposing this problem.

## k) Announcing Judgments

God raised up the prophetic ministry to speak to evil people and nations and warn them of approaching judgments. God's purposes in judgment are clearer, if a prophet announces them in advance.

The prophet's declaration and intercession gives God authority to deal with evil. When a situation turns sour and God needs to take action, his prophets announce his condemnation of the evil. This prophetic declaration gives him permission to send a judgment event against the evil that the prophet had pronounced judgment against. The prophet's declaration expresses God's verdict on the evil. God's action against evil represents his sentence against it.

Prophets and judgments go together. Without the prophets, God does not have authority to bring preventive judgments against evil. Unless God sends judgments against emerging evil, the prophets would be just crying in the wind. Prophets and judgments are God's strategy for constraining evil in the world.

*When a people reach a certain level of moral depravity, punishment ceases to be particular and becomes national. The civil order has lost its ability to act for God and God then acts against that order (RJ Rushdoony).*

The modern world thinks of judgment as a grumpy god going round whacking people. However, most people in the world do not get justice. Their life is full of injustice. Various empires and political leaders have promised to get them justice, but the ordinary people never receive it. Fair judgment is good news for most people.

If we want to understand God's judgement, we should read the Beatitudes. The poor will be blessed. The rich will be disappointed, because they have already received their comfort. Those who have had plenty and privilege might miss out.

## 1) Warning of Danger

When Paul was going up to Jerusalem the prophet Agabus warned him of danger that he would face when he arrived (Acts 21:10-11). God often prepares his people in this way. The prophet is a watchman, who warns God's people of coming trouble.

> Does a bird fall into a trap on the ground where no snare has been set? Does a trap spring up from the earth when there is nothing to catch? When a trumpet sounds in a city, do not the people tremble? When disaster comes to a city, has not the Lord caused it? Surely the Sovereign Lord does nothing without revealing his plan to his servants the prophets (Amos 3:5-7).

*The prophet must identify the fundamental evil of his generation. He must also identify, long in advance, the most likely specific evils that will consume the society and bring God's wrath (Gary North - Prophets, Leaders, Followers, Losers).*

*One element of Christian compassion is outrage. If we see what is wrong as God sees it, we will feel about it as God feels it. Moses was outraged when he looked on the burdens of his people. His nation was immature but his outrage was natural. In the time of the prophets, as Israel's national decadence brought in its wake violent social injustice and inhumanity the outrage of prophets is searing. Amos was furious when he saw the poor sold for the price of shoes (Os Guiness).*

The Lord warned Israel and Judah through all his prophets
and seers: "Turn from your evil ways" (2 Kings 17:13).

*It is the duty of God's servants to warn men of their danger, to point out
that their rebellion against God leads to certain destruction, and to call
them to flee from the wrath to come. It is their duty to rebuke wickedness
wherever it is found. Those who expose hypocrites, resist tyrants and
oppose the wicked, are over wielded by them as troublemakers. Those who
by their sins provoke God's wrath are the real troublesters, and not those
who warn them of the dangers to which their wickedness exposes them (A
W Pink).*

## m) Interpreting the Signs of the Times

Jesus criticised the Jews because they could understand the
weather, but could not interpret the signs of the times.

He said to the crowd: "When you see a cloud rising in the
west, immediately you say, 'It's going to rain,' and it does.
And when the south wind blows, you say, 'It's going to be
hot,' and it is. Hypocrites! You know how to interpret the
appearance of the earth and the sky. How is it that you
don't know how to interpret this present time?" (Luke
12:54-56).

Prophets must understand the signs of the times and
interpret them to the world.

*Within the long, circuitous, often delayed progress in understanding, there
were sudden explosions of saving activity..... It is to the prophets that
God revealed the coming and meaning of such times; indeed from one point
of view, the prophet may be described as the person who, more than anyone
else, knows what time it is (Robert - Banks - the Tyranny of Time).*

*The seer is made able to read the spiritual climate. He is made able to
identify the prevalent motivational force. His role is to see through masks
and veils of pretension, to expose man's folly and evil, for the sake of seeing
the poor and needy through. The watchman is set over men's hearts to
discern motivation, and to pray for and to call forth correction. The seer is
set over men's hearts to call them to heavenly living. The prophet is a seer.
The basic nature of his commission is observation and watchfulness. He is
prone to contemplation and skilled in the art of deduction (Lars
Widerberg - The Seer).*

*The seer is one who has understanding of the times. This person has the ability to perceive and discern the spiritual significance of a situation and can give the Lord's perspective on a given situation. This person's strengths are giftings of illumination and discernment, though they may or may not communicate what they see in any one set or particular manner. This kind of prophet is extremely valuable as a watchman and intercessor in the midst of the Church (Jim Wies - Different Kinds of Prophets).*

## n) The Meaning of History

Prophets have a role in explaining the meaning of history. When a culture loses its understanding of its history, it loses its sense of direction. God's plan for history is revealed through his prophets.

> In reading this, then, you will be able to understand my insight into the mystery of Christ, which was not made known to men in other generations as it has now been revealed by the Spirit to God's holy apostles and prophets (Eph 3:4-5).

*God's actions in human history had to be interpreted and this was one of the major roles of the prophets (Clifford Hill - Shaking the Nations).*

## o) Testing of Prophecy

Prophets are called to speak God's word. Another important part of their ministry, which we need to see developed, is testing prophecy.

> Two or three prophets should speak, and the others should weigh carefully what is said (1 Cor 14:29).

Part of the prophetic role is to sit and listen to prophecies and "weigh carefully" the words that are spoken. Several prophets should do this together. If a prophecy does not get a consensus support, it should be discarded.

Testing prophecies is an important aspect of the prophetic ministry. We are now hearing more and more prophetic words being spoken to the church, but the quality is still very mixed. Christians do not know which words should be taken seriously.

Many warnings of disaster have not been fulfilled. This unclear sounding of the trumpet is producing confusion in the church. The solution is to get prophets more involved in testing of prophecies and sorting the wheat from the chaff.

## p) Watchman
Some prophets are watchmen who stand on the walls of the city of God to see what God is doing. They look into the distance to see what is coming. They often see a long way ahead. Several scriptures describe the role of the watchman.

> The prophet, along with my God, is the watchman over Ephraim, yet snares await him on all his paths, and hostility in the house of his God (Hos 9:8).

> I have posted watchmen on your walls, O Jerusalem; they will never be silent day or night. You who call on the Lord, give yourselves no rest (Is 62:6).

> Israel's watchmen are blind, they all lack knowledge; they are all mute dogs, they cannot bark; they lie around and dream, they love to sleep (Is 56:10).

> I appointed watchmen over you and said, 'Listen to the sound of the trumpet!' But you said, 'We will not listen' (Jer 6:17).

Ezekiel was called to be a watchman.

> The word of the Lord came to me: "Son of man, speak to your countrymen and say to them: 'When I bring the sword against a land, and the people of the land choose one of their men and make him their watchman, and he sees the sword coming against the land and blows the trumpet to warn the people, then if anyone hears the trumpet but does not take warning and the sword comes and takes life, his blood will be on his own head. Since he heard the sound of the trumpet but did not take warning, his blood will be on his own head. If he had taken warning, he would have saved himself. But if the watchman sees the sword coming and does not blow the trumpet to warn the people and the sword comes and takes the life of one of them. I will hold the watchman accountable (Ezek 33:1-6).

The prophet was called a watchman because his role in the spiritual realm is the same as a literal watchman in the natural realm. Watchmen were stationed at specific posts on the walls of the city that gave them the visibility to watch for the king or other members of the nobility to announce their coming. They also looked for enemies coming from a distance and disorder arising within the city.

> *These watchmen were especially trained to be able to distinguish the enemy from their brethren. Only those with the best vision and judgement were given these posts. They could not be overly prone to sound the alarm, or to request that the gates be opened. They had to be accurate in their discernment. If there were too many false alarms the people would begin to disregard them. If they were careless and let an enemy in the gate, they could jeopardise the entire city. This was an extremely crucial position for which accuracy and dependability were required (Rick Joyner - The Ministry of a Watchman).*

> *The seer is marked by intellectual capacity and maturity. Spiritual gifting neither guarantees truth nor constitutes maturity (Lars Widerberg - The Seer).*

## q) Challenging the Nations

The primary responsibility of the prophets is to speak to the people of God. They bring both direction and correction to the Church. But prophets may also be called to speak to their nation. Many of the prophets of the Old Testament found themselves confronting kings, and taking an important role in national affairs. Some also addressed their words to foreign nations. Isaiah, Jeremiah and Ezekiel each prophesied to the surrounding nations.

> *The prophets of Israel did not live in isolation—they were acutely aware of international politics and the rise and fall of nations. Some of them pronounced messages against the nations of their times. All of them were concerned about the world situation, and it was part of their calling to issue prophecies against the other nations of the world (Milton Smith).*

*Having matured in their prophetic gifting through years of faithful obedience to God, prophets will begin to operate on new levels of prophetic authority. Worldwide, prophets will speak before civil governments, delivering powerful prophetic speeches to nations, literally shaking their existing political foundations (Dennis Cramer - Prophetic Power).*

## r) Initiating God's Action

God does nothing without warning his people first. Part of the prophetic role is to release God's activity by providing these warnings (Amos 3:7). Isaiah spoke of God stretching out his hand according to his plan.

> The Lord Almighty has sworn, "Surely, as I have planned, so it will be, and as I have purposed, so it will stand... This is the plan determined for the whole world; this is the hand stretched out over all nations. For the Lord Almighty has purposed, and who can thwart him? His hand is stretched out, and who can turn it back?" (Is 14:24-27).

*Prophetic hearts, not prophetic charts, will change the course of history and bring God's prophesied will into actual effect (Philip Greenslade - The Sharp Cutting Edge).*

## s) Theology

Prophets should be experts on God. Part of their role is to pass on theological and biblical insights to the church. A prophet should also be an amateur theologian.

## t) Healing the Sick

Some prophets are used in healing the sick. Elijah was a prophet who moved effectively in the gift of healing. Elisha followed in his mentor's footsteps.

> When Elisha reached the house, there was the boy lying dead on his couch. He went in, shut the door on the two of them and prayed to the Lord. Then he got on the bed and lay upon the boy, mouth to mouth, eyes to eyes, hands to hands. As he stretched himself out upon him, the boy's body grew warm. Elisha turned away and walked back and forth in the room and then got on the bed and stretched out upon him once more. The boy sneezed seven times and opened his eyes (2 Kings 4:32-35).

## u) Appointing and Anointing Leaders

In Old Testament times, God often used a prophet to appoint and anoint national leaders. Samuel anointed Saul, and then David, as King. A prophet anointed Solomon as his successor.

Elijah was told to anoint Jehu son of Nimshi king over Israel (1 Kings 19:16).

In a godly nation, prophets may have a role in the appointment of civil leaders. Prophets also have a role in anointing other prophets for ministry.

> Anoint Elisha son of Shaphat from Abel Meholah to succeed you as prophet. So Elijah went from there and found Elisha son of Shaphat. He was plowing with twelve yoke of oxen, and he himself was driving the twelfth pair. Elijah went up to him and threw his cloak around him (1 Kings 19:16, 19).

## v) Advising Kings and Political Rulers

Prophets have a role in providing advice to kings and rulers. When God wanted to give guidance to a ruler, he often gave it through a prophet. David had the prophets Nathan and Gad in his palace. They advised him about a whole range of issues (2 Sam 7:1-4,17).

> But the prophet Gad said to David, "Do not stay in the stronghold. Go into the land of Judah." So David left and went to the forest of Hereth (1 Sam 22:5).

> So Gad went to David and said to him, "Shall there come upon you three years of famine in your land? Or three months of fleeing from your enemies while they pursue you? Or three days of plague in your land? Now then, think it over and decide how I should answer the one who sent me" (2 Sam 24:13).

A prophet advised Ahab as he went into battle.

> Meanwhile a prophet came to Ahab king of Israel and announced, "This is what the Lord says: 'Do you see this vast army? I will give it into your hand today, and then you will know that I am the Lord'".... The man of God

> came up and told the king of Israel, "This is what the Lord says, I will deliver this vast army into your hands, and you will know that I am the Lord" (1 Kings 20:13,28).

Elisha provided guidance to the army of Israel that frustrated its enemies.

> The man of God sent word to the king of Israel: "Beware of passing that place, because the Arameans are going down there." So the king of Israel checked on the place indicated by the man of God. Time and again Elisha warned the king, so that he was on his guard in such places (2 Kings 6:9-10).

## w) Historian

Prophets will often be historians, as their interest in the future rolls over into an interest in the past. Some of the Bible was written by prophets recording the works of God.

> As for the events of King David's reign, from beginning to end, they are written in the records of Samuel the seer, the records of Nathan the prophet and the records of Gad the seer, together with the details of his reign and power, and the circumstances that surrounded him and Israel and the kingdoms of all the other lands (1 Chron 29:29-30).

> The other events of Uzziah's reign, from beginning to end, are recorded by the prophet Isaiah son of Amoz (2 Chron 26:22).

## x) Guiding Angels

Angels are ministering spirits sent to serve God's children (Heb 1:14). They are sent by God to serve God's people.

> Bless the Lord, you His angels,
> Who excel in strength,
> who do His word,
> Heeding the voice of His word (Psalm 103:20).

Angels are created for obedience. They do not have the friendship with God that is opened up to us through the presence of the Holy Spirit. Angels often do not know as much about what is on the Father's heart as we do. They often "excel in strength" far more than they excel in wisdom and decision-making.

Angels move between heaven and earth. When they are in heaven, they know what God is doing, because his Kingdom is established there. When they are on earth, they are dependent on other messengers from heaven to keep them up-to-date with what God is doing.

Angels are sent to earth to serve us, but as events develop, they often do not know what to do next. They sometimes have to wait for our prophetic declarations before they know what to do. When they hear the Holy Spirit's word through us, they do it. They recognise his voice and obey it. They listen to a prophetic word and work to accomplish it. That is one reason why God does nothing without first revealing his plan to his servants the prophets (Amos 3:7). Speaking in the language of angels is good (1 Cor 13:1), because it helps the angels to know what the Holy Spirit is saying.

## y) Explaining What Must Be Done

Many prophets are warning of future disastrous events, but very few are explaining what God is doing and how he will work through these events to bring change. Focusing on the darkness prevents them from seeing what Jesus is seeing. A related problem is that many Christians seem to enjoy warnings of judgement on the world, more than they want strategies that would require them to take action to bring in the victory of God.

God does not cause troubles and calamities; they are rooted in human evil or folly, with a bit of demonic mischief thrown in. During a judgement, God takes this human mess and works it for good to achieve his purposes.

One role of the prophet is to warn of troubles before they come, so God's people can prepare. Their more important task is to explain what God is doing through the event, so his people can participate in his purposes. Prophets can only accomplish this task, if they are standing outside the dark cloud of human events and seeing with the eyes of Jesus.

When a prophet receives a warning of a calamitous event, their task has just begun. The next step is to find out what God plans to achieve through the event, and his strategy for the people who want to participate in his purposes during that event. We need more of the eyes of Jesus and less of the gloom.

> If your gift is prophesying, then prophesy in accordance
> with your faith (Romans 12:6).

Christians with the gift of prophesying should prophesy in proportion to their faith. Prophesying judgment to a nation in decline does not take much faith. Prophesying the strategy by which God will use the judgement to change the nation and bring a great victory takes much more faith. That is a challenge for modern prophets.

*God has always had His specialists whose chief concern has been the moral breakdown and the decline in the spiritual health of the nation or the church. Such men were Elijah, Jeremiah, Malachi and others of their kind who appeared at critical moments in history to reprove, rebuke, and exhort in the name of God and righteousness. Such a man was likely to be drastic, radical, possibly at times violent, and the curious crowd that gathered to watch him work soon branded him as extreme, fanatical, negative. And in a sense they were right. He was single-minded, severe, fearless, and these were the qualities the circumstances demanded. He shocked some, frightened others and alienated not a few, but he knew who had called him and what he was sent to do. His ministry was geared to the emergency, and that fact marked him out as different, a man apart (A W Tozer).*

# 4

# Prophet to the Nation

**Levels of Activity**
Prophets can minister at different levels.

**1. People**
Some prophets specialise in speaking to individual people.
Personal prophecy provides:

- guidance
- correction

**2. Church**
Other prophets speak primarily to their church.  Prophets
provide a church with:

- guidance
- vision
- warnings

Loren Cunningham said that pastors are like wet cement.
They are very accepting and draw everything together.  He
said that prophets are like reinforcing steel.  They give the
concrete strength by keeping it pure.  A strong building
needs both cement and steel.

## 3. The Nations

Some Christians will be called to be a prophet to their nation.
They may also develop the ability to speak to other nations.
A prophet to a nation provides:

- advice to rulers
- interpretation of God's law
- warning of judgement.

## Prophet to the Nation

The primary responsibility of a prophet is to bring direction
and correction to their church, but God may raise some
prophets up to be a prophet to their nation. Many of the
prophets of the Old Testament found themselves
confronting kings, and taking an important role in national
affairs. Some also addressed their words to foreign nations.
They demonstrate the ministry of the Prophet to the Nation.

## Times of Transformation

A Prophet to the Nation releases God's hand of power. We
are living in a time of transformation, when God's purposes
will be accomplished through "shaking" and judgement. The
ministry of the prophet is very important at these times,
because God cannot act, without first giving a warning
through his prophets.

> Surely the Sovereign Lord does nothing without revealing
> his plan to his servants the prophets (Amos 3:7).

God cannot shake a nation until he has announced it
through his prophets. There are two reasons for this.

First, God is merciful and always gives people an
opportunity to repent, before he sends judgement on a
nation. God would be happier if he did not have to shake
the nation, so he gives a warning, hoping that his people will
put things right. But if the warning is not heeded, God has
no alternative but to act himself.

Second, any shaking must be recognised as coming from the hand of God. If a judgement is seen as a normal event, it can be ignored. An event that has been announced beforehand by God's servants is obviously a work of God and its meaning will be clear. The fact that it has been announced beforehand proves that it is a work of God.

*The prophet knows what time it is, knows what kind of time it is. He holds prophetic understanding of the mentality and mood of this present time. He identifies and knows the trends of a society by looking at its roots. He is able to analyse trends and upcoming events by judging foundations. His words are a force against the mentality of the day (Lars Widerburg - The Forthtellers).*

*Prophets see more than others the continuing influences that issue from the past and profoundly affect the present and the ultimate future. They see the continuum, the unbroken span of past, present and future as few see it (Art Katz - What is the Prophetic Church).*

## Changing Governments

The story of Abimelech contrasts three different methods of bringing political change (Judges 9). Two bring bad results.

## 1. Democracy

Abimelech was elected by a democratic process, but he did great harm to the people of Shechem. This incident is a timely reminder that democracy gives power to the wrong people. The skills needed to get ahead in politics are pragmatism, arrogance and a light hand on the truth. These are very different from the skills needed by a good judge.

## 2. Rebellion

A rebellion against an evil leader will usually fail, because violence produces violence. A person capable of rebellion is also capable of being a dictator.

Now Gaal son of Ebed moved with his brothers into Shechem, and its citizens put their confidence in him....
Then Gaal son of Ebed said, "Who is Abimelech, and who is Shechem, that we should be subject to him? If only this

people were under my command! Then I would get rid of him" (Jud 9:26,28,29).

Gaal led a rebellion, but he and those who followed him were destroyed (Jud 9:38-41).

## 3. Prophetic Proclamation

This best way to remove a bad government is prophetic proclamation. When a prophetic voice speaks God's judgment against an evil ruler, God will honour that word and bring sanctions against the wicked person. Jothan, the youngest brother escaped and prophesied against Abimelech and the people of Shechem.

> If then you have acted honorably and in good faith ... may Abimelech be your joy, and may you be his too! But if you have not, let fire come out from Abimelech and consume you, citizens of Shechem and Beth Millo, and let fire come out from you, citizens of Shechem and Beth Millo, and consume Abimelech (Jud 9:19-20).

God honoured this prophetic word.

> After Abimelech had governed Israel three years, God sent an evil spirit between Abimelech and the citizens of Shechem, who acted treacherously against Abimelech (Jud 9:22-23).

Abimelech was removed by prophecy.

> Thus God repaid the wickedness that Abimelech had done.... God also made the men of Shechem pay for all their wickedness. The curse of Jotham... came on them (Jud 9:56-57).

Modern Christians place a lot of faith in democracy, even though it does not produce godly government. Others have tried rebellion, but this has failed too. Prophetic proclamation is the best way to get rid of an evil government. Unfortunately, belief that God can bring governments down is rare. The missing element is a strong prophetic voice to release God's power to bring political change.

## Prophets and Tyranny

One reason that tyranny has been so serious in the twentieth century is the lack of prophets among the nations. There have been no prophets challenging political rulers to obey God. Many rulers do not even know that they are required to serve God, or that he has put limits on their jurisdiction. God can only act against evil rulers, if he has a prophet to speak out his challenge and warn of his judgements (Amos 3:7). God will not bring sanctions against wicked rulers unless their sins are clearly understood.

If the prophets have not announced the judgement in advance, the rulers will not understand that it was sent by God. They will not realise that the calamity is the consequence of their sins. They will assume that it is just another tragic event. Some rulers may even use the trouble to expand their powers. If a judgement is not announced in advance by the prophets, its purpose is diffused or lost.

> *Amos was not welcomed in his own society. When a genuine prophet arrives on the scene, he tends to make people uncomfortable. The people of Amos' day were affluent and religiously devout- as well as being military secure and governmentally sound. The last thing they wanted was a prophet to meddle their well-ordered lives (Bob Munford).*

Isaiah 16 describes a number of kings and tyrants, who were brought down from the place of pride and power by the shaking of God. He gave relief from suffering and cruel bondage by destroying the aggressive and oppressive rulers. God was able to stretch forth his hand and accomplish his purpose, because prophets like Isaiah had prophesied.

The worst thing that can happen to a nation is to have no prophets. The cry of a people under tyranny is awful.

> We are given no miraculous signs; no prophets are left, and none of us knows how long this will be... Will the foe revile your name forever? Why do you hold back your hand, your right hand? Take it from the folds of your garment and destroy them! (Psalm 74:9-11).

The Psalmist feels like his nation is in a hopeless situation. It is being ruled by a tyrant and God's hand of judgement against this injustice is being held back. The Psalmist knows that God has power to destroy the wicked ruler, but while there are no prophets, this is unlikely to happen.

A Prophet to the Nation will have to emerge in the church first, but the modern church has been unwilling to release this gift. The prophetic ministry has been stifled in the church, so the Prophet to the Nation has been rare. The absence of the prophetic ministry has impoverished the church, but it has had even more serious consequences for the world. Tyrants have been able to rule with impunity, as God's hand of judgement has been held back, hidden in his garment, the church.

## Restraining the Sword

The sword is dangerous and the political sphere will always tend to expand. People with political power will always see new problems to solve and people expecting them to solve them. Rulers are always tempted to expand their power.

Pressure on the state to do more good is dangerous, because the state can use force to expand its role. This is a great dilemma for political theory. The state needs force to punish criminals and protect society. However, this monopoly on force makes it almost impossible for citizens to prevent their government from expanding its power. We cannot resist the state, because it is stronger than we are.

History suggests that this is a serious problem. Throughout the twentieth century, the power of the state, whether dictator or democracy, has increased immensely. Even where political powers start out with modest intentions, they seem to end up with more power and control. Democracy does not prevent this from happening, but tends to make the situation worse. It tends to produce leaders who pander to the desires of the people.

## Prophetic Antidote

The only antidote to the expanding state is Christian prophets proclaiming the law in partnership with God. When the church is functioning correctly, God will raise up Prophets to the Nation, who can speak his word to its rulers. These prophets will confront their rulers, whenever they take up power and responsibility that does not belong to them.

Biblical law sets out the boundaries on the power of the state. Prophets to the Nation will challenge any political ruler who takes powers that are not authorised by the law. If the rulers do not heed these warnings, the prophets will announce God's judgement against them. If the rulers then persist in taking power that God has not given to them, they will experience his judgement. If they will not voluntarily shrink their power to the size specified by God, he will cut them down to size. The law and the prophets are the key to limiting the power of the state (Rom 3:21).

This earth belongs to the Lord, so all rulers are his servants. They do not have absolute power. If they take power that has not been delegated to them, they are in rebellion against him. When a ruler ignores God's will, the prophets will warn of God's judgement. If the rulers refuse to surrender to God, they can expect his sanctions to fall upon them. The best restraint on the power of the sword is the power of the trumpet.

> About that time Jeroboam was going out of Jerusalem, and Ahijah the prophet of Shiloh met him on the way, wearing a new cloak. The two of them were alone out in the country, and Ahijah took hold of the new cloak he was wearing and tore it into twelve pieces. Then he said to Jeroboam, "Take ten pieces for yourself, for this is what the Lord, the God of Israel, says: 'See, I am going to tear the kingdom out of Solomon's hand and give you ten tribes'" (1 Kings 11:29-31).

Solomon had rejected God's word by taking foreign wives to form alliances with foreign nations. Ahijah announced God's judgement against Solomon. This resulted in his son Rehoboam losing most of the kingdom to another king.

## Crisis and Hope

In the troubled times that lie ahead many people will have their hope shattered. The plans and the projects to which they have given their lives will collapse. They will often feel as if God has abandoned them. The nations will need prophets who can give new vision during these times of shaking.

> *We must recognise the danger of despair that comes with extinguishing dreams. In the troubled times that lie ahead many will believe that their dreams have died. Theologically they will believe that God has abandoned them. If the church in our time is to avoid despair we must construct the new vision of God's presence in the midst of our judgement (Bruce Bint).*

> *With the shattering changes—political, economic and technological -that have been thrust upon the twentieth century world it is a small wonder that the generation facing the close of the second millennium and peering uncertainly into the uncharted waters of the twenty first century are crying out for divine guidance (Clifford Hill - Prophecy, Past and Present).*

Prophets will explain how God is at work in what appears to be a disaster and give direction and hope for the future. When Israel was in trouble and needed a deliverer, God sent a prophet.

> They invaded the land to ravage it. Midian so impoverished the Israelites that they cried out to the Lord for help. When the Israelites cried to the Lord because of Midian, he sent them a prophet (Jud 6:5-8).

## God's Spokesperson

A Prophet to the Nation is a person who speaks on behalf of God. Peter said that prophecy never had its origin in the will of man, but men spoke from God as they were carried along by the Holy Spirit.

> Above all, you must understand that no prophecy of Scripture came about by the prophet's own interpretation. For prophecy never had its origin in the will of man, but men spoke from God as they were carried along by the Holy Spirit (2 Pet 1:20-21).

They were moved by the Spirit, so they could speak in the name of the Lord. When calling Jeremiah, God said he would put his words in the prophet's mouth. The Lord said to him,

> You must go to everyone I send you to and say whatever I command you… I have put my words in your mouth (Jer 1:7,9).

The same point is made in Deuteronomy 18:18:

> I will raise up a prophet… I will put my words in his mouth and he will tell them everything that I command him.

Prophets speak in obedience to the Lord. They say only what God tells them to say. They bring God's word to the church and the world. Ezekiel described this as the Lord's hand being upon him.

> The hand of the Lord was upon me (Ezek 37:1).

> *The prophet of God was thus the mouthpiece of God. He was God's messenger whose task was to deliver whatever God said to him. He was not simply a holy man, nor was he a man with a mission to reform the world or to accomplish any particular task of religious teaching or leadership. The Prophet was simply a "mouthpiece" (Clifford Hill - Prophecy, Past and Present).*

A prophet is defined as much by willingness to speak as ability to hear. Every Christian should be able to hear God. However, only a few have the courage and boldness to speak everything that God wants spoken. Prophets have a special sense of the heart and burdens of God. They are committed to the truth. They are willing to speak God's word, regardless of the cost. God needs prophets who will speak his word fearlessly, without regard to the consequences.

> You must speak my words to them, whether they listen or fail to listen (Ezek 2:7).

*They developed a keen sense of God's presence and knew when he wanted to speak to his people. They sensed his moods and his burdens of heart, even before they knew exactly what they were feeling. It was wonderful, but it also confused them because they often felt squeezed between what God wanted to do and the religious routine going on about them (Stephen L Mansfield – Pastoring the Prophetic).*

The task of the prophet is demonstrated in the relationship between Moses and Aaron. Moses was not a good speaker, so God said Aaron would be his "prophet". He explained what this would mean.

> You shall speak to him and put words in his mouth…. He will speak to the people for you, and it will be as if he were your mouth and as if you were God to him (Ex 4:15-16).

## Prophet for the Season

Every prophet is different and unique. We should not try to fit them all into the same mould. God always has the right person for the time and season.

*Jeremiah was God's man for a nation flying apart (David Pawson).*

*In this connection we must remember that the entire prophetic institution was a gift from God. It was not an expression of the religious nature of the people, but a divine gift. The prophets were raised up of God: they did not emerge from the national religious consciousness. As the spokesman of God they uttered their messages wherever God commanded them to do so (Edward J Young - My Servants the Prophets).*

## Eyes of the Nation

There is a watching aspect to the ministry of a prophet. In fact one of the words for prophet is the Hebrew word Seer.

> Formerly in Israel, if a man went to inquire of God, he would say, "Come, let us go to the seer," because the prophet of today used to be called a seer (1 Sam 9:9).

*Seers are men of revelation. Seers are men of enlightenment. Seers are men of intellectual maturity…. The prophet is a seer. The basic nature of his commission is observation and watchfulness. He is prone to contemplation and skilled in the art of deduction (Lars Widerberg - The Seer).*

Isaiah described the prophets as the "eyes" of the nation.

> The Lord has brought over you a deep sleep:
> He has sealed your eyes (the prophets);
> he has covered your heads (the seers) (Is 29:10).

Balaam was a false prophet, yet the Lord used him when the Spirit came on him. He spoke the truth when he said a prophet needed open eyes to see what God is doing.

> The oracle of Balaam son of Beor, the oracle of one
> whose eye sees clearly, the oracle of one who hears the
> words of God, who sees a vision from the Almighty, who
> falls prostrate, and whose eyes are opened (Num 24:4).

Prophets are people of vision, who can see what God is doing. They co-operate with God in breaking down all that is not built on the true foundation. They do this by announcing his judgements. At the same time, they watch over all that God is doing in the nation to ensure it is built according to his Word.

> *The prophet does not confuse truth with consensus. The prophet does not confuse God's word with the word of those who happen to hold power at present, or with the opinion of the majority. This is because powerholders and the majority can fall victim to a lying spirit—and this means a power that actually seizes the majority of experts, the political leadership, and the public (Michael Welker - God the Spirit).*

## Nations and Encouragement

Personal prophecy should be mostly encouragement. A problem occurs when a person who is fluent with the gift of prophecy and experienced with personal prophecy moves up to the role of prophet to a city or nation or state. These entities have a strong tendency to turn away from God, so they rarely need encouragement and mostly need warning and correction. Christians living within them need a clear trumpet sound to know what they should do.

> If the trumpet makes an uncertain sound,
> who will prepare for battle (1 Cor 14:8)?

73

Christians who have learned their craft bringing personal prophecies often try to step up and bring prophecies to their nation. If they do not understand the difference and make a transition to the different level of operation, they will often bring spiritual "warm fuzzies" when the nation really needs a clear trumpet call.

In a prophecy to any nation, at least a couple of these questions should be answered.

- What is going on in this nation?
- Has the season changed?
- What do the people of the nation or its leaders need to do to turn things around?
- What is God doing in the nation?
- What do the people of God need to do, to be a part of what the Lord is doing?

None of these questions refer to predictions about the future? However, it is more important to know what God is doing now and what his people should be doing now, than what will happen in the future. Knowing who will be the next President will not help us at all, if we do not understand what is happening in the nation that has allowed God to give us a particular President.

Most prophecies on the internet for nations do not measure up. They just carry on the encouragement model that is typical of personal prophecy. This will provide plenty of spiritual garbage, but a clear trumpet call is rare.

*Mere preachers may help anybody and hurt nobody: but prophets will stir everybody and madden somebody. The preacher goes with the crowd; the prophet goes against it. A man freed, fired, and filled with God will be branded unpatriotic because he speaks against his nations sins; unkind because his tongue is a two edged sword, unbalanced because the weight of preaching opinion is against him. The preacher will be heralded, the prophet will be hounded (L Ravenhill - Why Revival Tarries).*

## Moral Campaigners

God does not call Christians to be "moral campaigners". The Pharisees were the moral campaigners of Jesus time. They loved to find fault with the weak and sinful people in their society, but Jesus criticised them for their lack of mercy and their spiritual blindness. He showed mercy to those trapped in the grip of sin.

The Pharisees got things wrong. They could not see their own sin, so they seemed like hypocrites. They dealt harshly with weak people who had been seduced by a culture of sin and were not clever enough to hide it, but missed the far more serious sins of society's leaders. They focused on obvious sexual sins, but were blinded to the more deceptive sins that open the nation to evil. This should be a serious warning to those who campaign against sin.

God does not need moral campaigners, but he does call a few of his people to speak prophetically to the nation. These prophets will remind the nation of God's standards and warn of the consequences for society. A key part of their role is to identify the core evils that are the root of their society's problems. They will not be obsessed with the more obvious sexual sins, but will focus on the subtle shifts in attitude that creep in and open the door to real evil. They will know that the sins of their political and cultural leaders are usually well hidden, but are really harmful.

True prophets will be concerned about devious and influential sins, like pride, selfishness and "state idolatry". They will be less concerned about sexual sins, as these generally only emerge when other more subtle sins have already taken hold in society. Blatant sexual sin is a symptom of a sick world, but is not generally the root cause. Prophets will be more concerned about the cause than the symptoms. They will focus on the sins that are destroying their society.

## Focus on the Cause not the Symptom

Much modern prophecy is shallow. Real prophets go deep to the heart of an issue. They are not distracted by surface issues and symptoms that that are not the real cause of what is happening. Prophets press in deeper until they get to the crux of the issues that are shaping the heart of their nation.

Abortion is an example of this problem. Most Christians realise that abortion is a sin. Some get really stirred up about it, but this prevents them from seeing the real issues affecting their nation. Abortion is not a legal issue, but a manifestation of a much deeper spiritual malaise. Something is seriously wrong with the spirit of the nation when many young women feel compelled to destroy their future heirs.

Prophetic people are wasting energy when they attempt to make abortion illegal, because banning abortion deals with the symptoms of the problem, but does not change the underlying cause that is rooted deep in the culture. The prophetic task is to expose the cracks in the heart of the nations that are manifesting through abortion. The solution is not a change in the law, but deep-seated repentance, a renewed world view, and powerful healing by God.

Abortion is just one manifestation of an impaired spirit. The Left Behind phenomena is another. Many Christians have lost confidence in the future and are looking to Jesus to come and rescue them soon. They have no confidence in the ability of the Holy Spirit to establish the Kingdom. This lack of faith puts them in danger of being cut off from their future, just as the young woman who has an abortion cuts off her own future. Abortion and rapture obsession result from the same spiritual flaw.

Many Christians are stirred up about homosexual marriage, but again they are focussing on the symptoms and not the root cause. Christian prophets will realise that homosexuality is a symptom and not the real crack in the heart of their culture. Ezekiel understood this issue well. When describing the sin of Sodom, he said.

> Now this was the sin of your sister Sodom: She and her daughters were arrogant, overfed and unconcerned; they did not help the poor and needy (Ezek 16:49).

Sodom's root sin was not homosexuality, but arrogance, laziness and refusal to care for the poor. It seems that when a society makes an idol of comfort and pleasure, it descends into a promiscuity that eventually manifests in homosexuality. What Lot found in Sodom was just the natural outcome for a society that worshipped comfort and wealth.

Lot saw the symptoms of the problem and like many Christians was upset about what he saw. Ezekiel looked much deeper and realised that the real issue was a love of comfort and pleasure. We need more prophets like Elijah who can see deep into the heart of their nation.

## Political Loyalties

Political loyalties are limiting for prophetic people. A person who is loyal to the right or the left will be able to function as a prophet in their church, but they are unlikely to move on to the role of prophet to their nation. Many will have had a strong interest in politics when they were young and may have strong political loyalties. They will have to drop their human loyalty and replace it with a loyalty to God.

Unless prophetic people understand that political parties and human politics are not part of God's plan, very few real prophets to the nations will emerge. Prophets cannot afford to be blinded by loyalty to a party or political leader.

People with valid prophetic gifts become "court prophets" when their loyalty to a particular political leader or his party takes precedence over their loyalty to God. The court prophets that led Jehoshaphat astray were not prophets of Baal. They were prophets of the Lord, trained among the sons of the prophets. They would have been brought to the palace when their ability to hear and speak the word of God was recognised, but they gradually became too loyal to the king's party. This prevented them from hearing clearly and left them vulnerable to a lying spirit (1 Kings 22).

Most modern nations do not have a clear prophetic voice. That is a dangerous place to be. I am sure that God is calling many of his people to be prophets to their nation. Unfortunately most are so wrapped up in politics that they cannot offer the total loyalty that God needs for this role. Blind loyalty to the left or right is blocking the prophetic flow at the national level.

## True Justice

Social justice is becoming an important issue for the church. This is good, because God is concerned about justice. However, too often the justice that is proclaimed is merely human justice. The church tends to jump on the bandwagon that is being pushed by liberal humanists. Moreover, the message is too often spoken by committees or church officials, who have no real authority in the eyes of the world. Their voices get lost amongst all the other voices that are speaking into modern society. If the church is to have an impact in the area of social justice, it must raise up prophets to speak to the nation.

Prophets will proclaim the justice and righteousness of God. They will know the issues that are on his heart and understand how true peace can be established. Prophets will speak in the name of the Lord, so they will have tremendous authority. God will watch over their words to ensure that they come to pass. Many are calling for the church to be prophetic, but this is impossible without prophets.

*As Christians we believe that God is active in the world and that his word can be heard in the events of human history. We believe it is the church's duty to proclaim what God is doing and what he would have us do. So Amos of old denounced the selfish indifference of the rich and the unjust suffering of the poor in Israel. Jeremiah who proclaimed that the inevitable judgement of a just God on his faithless people was to be seen in the fall of Jerusalem.*

*We cannot doubt that God is at work in the turmoil of our world today, in inflation, in industrial unrest and political uncertainty, in the aspirations of the third world. He has a word for us to proclaim to our contemporaries, a word of challenge, of judgement, of comfort and of hope. Yet the voice of the church and of Christians generally seems, strangely silent. What a nation needs more than anything else is not a Christian ruler in the palace, but a Christian prophet in earshot (Kenneth Kaunda, Former President of Zambia).*

## Guidance to Rulers

A key role of a Prophet to a Nation is to provide guidance to rulers. Prophets will be experts on God's law, so they can teach political authorities how to obey it (Deut 17:18-19). The Prophet to the Nation will teach national leaders how to implement God's law. As prophets love the law more than others, they will have better understanding of its principles. Their wisdom will assist those who are struggling to interpret the law. Prophets will understand the principles of good government, so they will be able to provide good guidance to those in authority.

Leading a nation can be a frightening task. Many decisions have to be made and most of them are hard, so rulers have always attempted to surround themselves with wise people. The king of Israel knew the benefit of having a prophet close by to help him make decisions (2 Kings 6:8-12). Prophets will give supernatural guidance to political rulers. Because their wisdom is from God, it will be effective.

God establishes Prophets to the Nation by giving them the wisdom that rulers need. The King of Israel knew that Elisha was a prophet, because his words were useful. The King of Babylon trusted Daniel, because he interpreted a dream that none of the Babylonian wise men understood. This is a very important principle. Many people, including prophets, are willing to criticise their government.

Prophets to the Nation are different. They begin their careers by assisting their leaders in tricky situations. Ahab trusted Miciah's words, because he provided correct advice in the past (1 Kings 22:7-8). Rulers who hate God will be glad to have prophets around because they need their advice.

Prophets give warning to the rulers of nations when they are taking the wrong direction or taking authority that God has not given them. Strong prophets are the best protection against misguided political leaders.

Good rulers welcome correction. The prophet Nathan challenged David when he committed adultery and murder, but remained his friend. He had established his credibility with David much earlier, when the King was planning the temple (2 Sam 7). Every ruler needs a prophet like Nathan who can hear the voice of God and challenge his sins. Rulers are usually surrounded by people trying to "grease up" to them. In this environment, a prophetic friend is the best protection against the occupational hazard of pride. All rulers need a friend to speak God's word to them.

Prophets to the Nation will pray for their government. Samuel prayed all night when his friend King Saul fell from grace (1 Sam 15:11). Every political leader needs a friend of God who will intercede with this intensity. God is raising up prophetic people all over the world, to be a prophetic voice in their church. Hopefully a few of these will go on to prophesy to their nations.

## Prophets and Law

The Old Testament prophets were the guardians of God's law. They prosecuted kings for their failure to obey it. Every prophet speaking at the national level must use God's law as a standard for testing the behaviour and actions of rulers and kings. To be an effective voice to their nation, these prophets must have a sound understanding of God's law.

Prophets who are not rooted in God's law will end up following after some fashionable secular voice. They can easily become the servant of particular political party. Without a clear standard, prophets will be blown around by every wind of change. Prophets exercising the power of the trumpet must love the law.

> Oh, how I love your law! I meditate on it all day long
> Your commands make me wiser than my enemies,
> for they are ever with me.
> I have more insight than all my teachers,
> for I meditate on your statutes.
> I have more understanding than the elders
> for I obey your precepts (Psalm 119:97-100).

This message is seen as a call to love the scriptures, but that is not what the Psalmist says. He promised that a love of the law would give us greater wisdom than our teachers. Prophets should study the law with passion to understand how it applies to civil government in a modern society.

The Old Testament prophets were like legal prosecutors who charged Israel with failure to keep the law. They were so passionate for God's law they were willing to risk the wrath of wicked Kings when confronting their nations sin.

> I will speak of your statutes before kings and will not be put to shame, for I delight in your commands because I love them (Psalm 119:46-47).

Prophets will only be able to speak clearly to the rulers of their nation, if they love the law.

## Prophets and Judges

The prophets will have a role in exposing judges who are unjust. Micah challenged the judges of Jerusalem for accepting bribes.

> Her leaders judge for a bribe, her priests teach for a price,
> and her prophets tell fortunes for money (Mic 3:11).

Jeremiah warned the judges against protecting evil people and not establishing justice.

> How can you say, "We are wise, for we have the law of the Lord," when actually the lying pen of the scribes has handled it falsely? The wise will be put to shame; they will be dismayed and trapped. Since they have rejected the word of the Lord, what kind of wisdom do they have? From the least to the greatest, all are greedy for gain; prophets and priests alike, all practice deceit. Are they ashamed of their loathsome conduct? No, they have no shame at all; they do not even know how to blush. So they will fall among the fallen; they will be brought down when they are punished, says the Lord (Jer 8:8-12).

The prophets will expose judges not honouring the law.

For really difficult cases, judges should call in people with spiritual discernment or prophetic insight (Deut 17:8-9). However, no matter how wise our judges, mistakes will be made. Judges should be humble, knowing that we will never get perfect justice on this earth. God is our final judge. When we stand before him, we will get perfect justice.

## Rare Ministry

A calling to speak as a Prophet to the Nation will be rare. Most prophets will function as an elder in a church and only a few will get the opportunity to prophesy to their nation. We should not confuse these two roles. Prophets with a recognised ministry in their church should not presume to be a Jeremiah or an Amos. Many of the more solemn and serious teachings in this book only apply to the Prophet to the Nation.

## Corruption

Prophets to the Nation must be careful not to be corrupted by their links with the state. Because they understand the art of government, they can be tempted to get involved in politics. Their responsibility is to speak God's word, so they must not usurp the role of the king. An excellent prophet would make an inferior king.

Prophets must not attempt to manipulate or control the civil authorities on God's behalf. They must speak God's word and leave the Holy Spirit to change the politician's heart. The key to being heard is to hear from God. Wise prophets will remain separate from the trappings of the state, so that they can speak with integrity.

Prophets to the Nation speak as individuals, not on behalf of their church. They will only have authority in their nation, if their words are true and anointed by the Holy Spirit.

*Ezekiel was not what we consider a normal person, but his abnormality is a key to his greatness, as has been the case with many of histories notable personality. Ezekiel's seems to have been a harsh ministry, but zeal to vindicate God and to preserve a remnant for mission proves him to have guided by profound insight. Among the truly great men of God stands this strange contradictory figure whose creative spirit, energised by God helped to return the mainstream of religion to its proper channel of mission. Ezekiel was a man of his times, and the time in which he lived was a time of great social, political and spiritual flux, that could have become either the basis for new creative understanding of the place of God in the life of man, or the dying of and inadequate faith. It was largely due to Ezekiel that out of the ashes of destruction came the resurrection of new faith and hope (Anonymous).*

*Some nations have a calling to be prophetic. They cannot achieve their destiny until the prophetic ministry is established in their midst (John Dawson).*

# 5

# The Watchman

A watchman belongs on the wall, looking out into the distant darkness to see if evil is coming and what God is doing. This can be lonely, discouraging work, but Jesus calls his guards to stay on the walls where they can see clearly.

Many watchmen are down in the city chatting with friends, because they got lonely. Others are on the conference circuit, where the money is better. Some are busy trolling the internet, but that is not the same as listening to the Lord. Others grew tired and have gone to sleep. Some have given up, because they are wearied by their warnings being rejected. The watchmen should not be in the city eating and drinking with the town's folk. They should be out on the watchtower looking into the night.

Jesus urgently needs his watchmen to get back up on the watchtower where he has appointed them.

> I have posted watchmen on your walls, O Jerusalem;
> they will never be silent day or night.
> You who call on the Lord, give yourselves no rest (Is 62:6).

> I appointed watchmen over you and said, "Listen to the sound of the trumpet!" But you said, "We will not listen" (Jer 6:17).

## Tower and Gate

God is restoring a watchman anointing. In biblical times, though a city had strong walls and double gates, security was not complete without watchmen in the watchtower, shouting, or heralding, anything they saw that was out of the ordinary. Their job was to warn the people of impending danger. They would pay with their lives if they failed to inform the city of an enemy's approach. If the watchmen were not alert, cities could fall, territories could be lost and many forced into captivity.

Watchmen are not on the walls to boost the name of the enemy and paralyse God's people with fear. Their purpose is to warn the people of danger, while it is still a long way off. This gives the people living outside the city time to get behind the walls where they will be safe. The guard's warning also gives the city leaders time to prepare their defences, so they can repel the enemy when it comes.

The safety of a city depends on the watchmen being on the watchtower. It also depends on the leaders at the gate heeding their warnings. If the watchmen and the leaders at the gate of the city each do their task, the enemy's plans should be defeated and the city kept safe.

*The watchmen were not the elders in the gates, nor did they have the authority to open or close the gates of a city. Neither did they have the authority to mobilise the militia against the enemy. Their job was to communicate what they saw to those who did have the authority.... They simply gave their information to the elders who sat in the gates. Only the elders had the authority to either command that the gates be opened or to sound the alarm (Rick Joyner - The Ministry of a Watchman).*

*The prophet is way ahead of the flock of sheep, perhaps five miles beyond the next hill. He is on the lookout. There he hears God's voice and sees visions, enters the throne-room of God and glimpses something (Wolfgang Simson - Houses That Changed the World).*

## Watchmen and Sheep

*A watchman was standing on a watchtower. He saw trouble coming and told the shepherds to get the sheep into the safety of the fold. The shepherd asked the watchman to get the sheep into the fold. However, when the watchman tried to round up the sheep, they just scattered. They did not know the voice of the watchman. Only when the shepherds heeded the watchman's warning and called the sheep did the sheep come into the fold.*

Watchmen stand on the walls of the city of God so that they can see what God is doing and call the people to respond. Good relationships between pastors and the watchman are essential. Watchman should speak their warnings to the pastors and elders, not to the people. The pastors should prepare their sheep for what the watchmen are seeing. The sheep know their shepherd and they will respond to their voice. If they do not know the voice of the prophets, they will not respond to them.

*The church has often lacked in having watchmen. She has had a type of watchman that has watched almost from a position on the floor of the church and not from the wall. The watchman is a prophet and as such is a seer and needs to be up high to see beyond the heights that even the king would see, since the king is not up the wall (Steve Snow - Eagle Watchman).*

## Embarrassing Parts

Those parts of the body that seem to be weaker are indispensable, and the parts that we think are less honorable we treat with special honor. And the parts that are unpresentable are treated with special modesty, while our presentable parts need no special treatment. But God has combined the members of the body and has given greater honor to the parts that lacked it, so that there should be no division in the body, but that its parts should have equal concern for each other (1 Cor 12:22-25).

Christians can be embarrassed by God's watchmen, as they seem to be intense, opinionated and scruffy. They may be the eyes of the body, but they are also the unseemly part that rids it of waste. If they are not functioning effectively in a church, it will be contaminated by garbage. So while they have an unseemly task, watchmen are important for the functioning of the body and deserve equal care and respect.

## Clear Sound

When a watchman receives a dream or vision about a cataclysmic event, they should give a clear warning.

> Again, if the trumpet does not sound a clear call, who will get ready for battle? (1 Cor 14:8).

A cataclysmic vision or dream may have any of the following possible meanings.

- a symbolic message with a spiritual interpretation,
- a warning of what Satan is planning,
- a warning event, that is a type of future evil,
- an event that may happen soon
- an event that is a long way into the future,
- an event that will only happen, if God's people do not repent.
- a final judgment on a people that has rejected God.

The response will be different for each type of revelation.

Modern Christians have a tendency to assume the worst. We generally interpret a vision or dream of awful events literally. We also assume that the event is coming soon and that its coming is certain. This is often not the case.

Sounding the trumpet is not sufficient. Sharing a vision is not enough. Watchmen are required to sound the trumpet clearly. When sharing a vision or dream, they should also explain its meaning. If this does not happen, God's people will become confused. Widespread confusion could lead to Christians being defeated and God's name being mocked.

During this current season, many visions are being shared. Most of these visions have come from the Lord, but their meaning has not been explained, so the people are confused.

## Gods Perspective

We must keep God's perspective in mind when interpreting warning visions. Christians often get so focused on the evil that Satan has planned that they fail to notice God's response. This gives Satan a place he does not deserve. He is a loser and all his schemes and plans will fail. Getting us absorbed in the negative part of a vision is his favourite trick for causing us to miss what God is saying and doing.

Focus on evil is the worst feature of the many "prophecy sites" on the internet. The bloggers and discussion groups get so absorbed in the evil being warned against, that they miss what God is saying and promising. We should fear God, not the devil and his schemes.

The watchman's task is not to make Christians afraid, but to show them how they can be victorious, if they prepare well. Most visions are not about the people of God being defeated, but are a promise that God's people can be victorious, if the watchmen do their work. We need watchmen who can tell us how to get ready. They will need to remove their "dark glasses" to fulfil their role.

Satan generally uses stealth and deception. The success of this strategy depends on Christians not waking up to what is happening until it is too late to respond. God counters by revealing Satan's plan's to the watchmen. They can then expose his plans and blow his cover.

*A watchman scans the horizon day and night. He must give a warning when danger is coming. If he does not see danger coming and warn the people, he will pay with this life. This is the cost of being a watchman (David Pawson).*

# 6
# Receiving the Word

There is only one way to receive a word from the Lord.

- Wait on the Lord
- Wait on the Lord
- Wait on the Lord
- Seek the Holy Spirit
- Seek the Holy Spirit
- Seek the Holy Spirit
- Pray
- Pray
- Read the Word
- Read the Word
- Read the Word
- Pray

To recognise a person's voice, you must know him well. Prophets must develop a strong relationship with God, so they can hear his voice. The key is waiting in the presence of the Lord and walking in the Spirit. We cannot tell the Lord when he should speak. We must wait for him. He is sovereign, so we must wait for him to speak (Jer 42:7).

## Listen to the Spirit

The angel said the following words to John seven times.

> He who has an ear, let him hear what the Spirit says to the churches (Rev 2:7).

Jesus said something similar at least four times.

> He who has ears, let him hear (Matt 13:9).

Listening and hearing are really important.

- The Spirit speaks. He speaks clearly in a language that we can know. He does not speak gobbledegook that we cannot understand.

- Prophets must listen to his voice. The Holy Spirit loves to speak and longs for his people to listen. The most important ability needed for serving God is to be able to hear the Spirit speak. If the prophets can hear him speak, everything falls into place.

- If the prophets cannot hear him, it is unlikely that he has stopped speaking. If they are getting confusion, the Spirit has not lost the plot. They are not listening correctly.

The most important skill is hearing the Holy Spirit speaking.

> I have much more to say to you, more than you can now bear. But when he, the Spirit of truth, comes, he will guide you into all truth. He will not speak on his own; he will speak only what he hears, and he will tell you what is yet to come. He will bring glory to me by taking from what is mine and making it known to you. All that belongs to the Father is mine. That is why I said the Spirit will take from what is mine and make it known to you (John 16:12-15).

## Different Ways

Different people and personalities hear God in different ways. Each prophet must find the way that is best for them.

> When the prophet of the Lord is among you, I reveal myself to him in visions I speak to him in dreams. But this is not true of my servant Moses; he is faithful in all my house with him I speak face to face; clearly and not in riddles; he sees the form of the Lord (Num 12:6-8).

A prophet can choose not to receive a word. Elisha did not want to seek a word of guidance for a wicked king.

> Elisha said to the king of Israel, "What do we have to do with each other? Go to the prophets of your father and the prophets of your mother" (2 Kings 3:13).

Sometimes worship or song may help the prophet to hear the Lord speak. Elisha used a harpist in this way.

> "But now bring me a harpist." While the harpist was playing, the hand of the Lord came on Elisha (2 Kings 3:15).

Prophets are expected to spend time in the presence of God. Jeremiah calls this "standing in the council of the Lord" to see or hear his word (Jer 23:18).

> *The prophetic ministry involves seeing things as they really are (Ian Breward).*

> *Prophets should not only be careful how they hear the Lord; they also need to learn that people's wishes can affect their hearing (John and Paula Sanford - The Elijah Task).*

## Wait

When a prophet has received a word from the Lord, the first thing they should do is ask what he wants them to do with it. They should not assume that he wants them to speak it out. He may want them to sit on it and wait and pray. They should also ask for an interpretation and guidance for how to deliver it. Many true words are spoiled, because they are incorrectly handled.

> *A prophetic minister must discipline himself to remain silent when God is silent (Mike Bickle - Growing in the Prophetic).*

A prophet loves to hear from God, but sometimes the message received can be painful to bear.

> I took the little scroll from the angel's hand and ate it. It tasted as sweet as honey in my mouth, but when I had eaten it, my stomach turned sour (Rev 10:10).

# 7

# Delivering Prophecy

Receiving a word from the Lord is the easy part of the prophetic ministry. The hardest part is learning how to communicate the word once it has been received. The Old Testament prophets communicated in a variety of ways. We have many more communication tools available today. We must learn how to use them in obedience to the Holy Spirit. If we can receive a word from him, we are capable of receiving guidance about how it should be communicated.

When the Holy Spirit gives a prophetic word, he usually gives instructions about how it should be delivered. Prophets must make sure that they get his instructions and act on them. A word that is delivered in an incorrect way is nullified, and effectively becomes a false prophecy.

*So a prophet needs to know more than what to say. He needs also to discover how God wants to him to say it (John and Paula Sanford - The Elijah Task).*

*Many times the biggest challenge for prophets is not necessarily in hearing the voice of God, but in learning how to minister the word in wisdom. This speaks of the timing, the manner, the place, the wording, the intent, the context, and the attitude of heart when ministering figures (Tom Hamon – The Spirit of Wisdom and Revelation).*

## Prophetic Methods

A word can be delivered in a variety of ways. We must be open to all the creativity of God in the delivery of his word. These are some of the methods that God uses:

### a) Speaking

The most common method for delivering a prophecy is for the prophet to speak directly to the recipients. God is a god who speaks. He can give instructions about the right time and the right place to speak, so getting the time and place correct is really important.

### b) Conversation

Sometimes a word will be spoken quietly to the person who needs it.

### c) Proxy

God may want another person to speak out the prophecy. When Jeremiah was in prison, he would dictate his words to Baruch who would read them to the king.

> Jeremiah called Baruch son of Neriah, and while Jeremiah dictated all the words the Lord had spoken to him, Baruch wrote them on the scroll (Jer 36:4).

### d) Preaching

A message from God may sometimes be given in a sermon. Some of the most prophetic words that I have heard were delivered as sermons.

### e) Writing

A word can be written down and delivered to the recipients. Isaiah and Jeremiah were writing prophets. The scriptures promise a blessing for those who read prophecy.

> Blessed is the one who reads the words of this prophecy, and blessed are those who hear it and take to heart what is written in it, because the time is near (Rev 1:3).

## f) Parables

Nathan told a story to get his message across to King David. He probably would not have received a direct word from Nathan.

> The Lord sent Nathan to David. When he came to him, he said, "There were two men in a certain town, one rich and the other poor. The rich man had a very large number of sheep and cattle, but the poor man had nothing except one little ewe lamb he had bought. He raised it, and it grew up with him and his children. It shared his food, drank from his cup and even slept in his arms. It was like a daughter to him. Now a traveller came to the rich man, but the rich man refrained from taking one of his own sheep or cattle to prepare a meal for the traveller who had come to him. Instead, he took the ewe lamb that belonged to the poor man and prepared it for the one who had come to him." David burned with anger against the man and said to Nathan, "As surely as the Lord lives, the man who did this deserves to die! He must pay for that lamb four times over, because he did such a thing and had no pity." Then Nathan said to David, "You are the man!" (2 Sam 12:1-7).

## g) Prophetic Action

Sometimes God asks a prophet to take an action that will illustrate the word being brought. The prophet becomes a living parable or visual aid. For example, Ezekiel lay on his side tied up with ropes for many days as a warning of the exile to Babylon (Ezek 4). Jeremiah bought a piece of land to bring home a prophetic message (Jer 32:1-9). Isaiah walked naked in the street to demonstrate the shame of Israel (Is 20). The key people can sometimes become actors in a living parable.

> By the word of the Lord one of the sons of the prophets said to his companion, "Strike me with your weapon," but the man refused. So the prophet said, "Because you have not obeyed the Lord, as soon as you leave me a lion will kill you." And after the man went away, a lion found him and killed him. The prophet found another man and said,

"Strike me, please." So the man struck him and wounded him. Then the prophet went and stood by the road waiting for the king. He disguised himself with his headband down over his eyes. As the king passed by, the prophet called out to him, "Your servant went into the thick of the battle, and someone came to me with a captive and said, 'Guard this man. If he is missing, it will be your life for his life, or you must pay a talent of silver.' While your servant was busy here and there, the man disappeared." "That is your sentence," the king of Israel said. "You have pronounced it yourself." Then the prophet quickly removed the headband from his eyes, and the king of Israel recognised him as one of the prophets. He said to the king, "This is what the Lord says: 'You have set free a man I had determined should die. Therefore it is your life for his life, your people for his people'" (1 Kings 20:35-42).

## h) Sealing the Word

Some words must be sealed up for delivery at a later time. Daniel was told to seal up some of his words for the future.

> He replied, "Go your way, Daniel, because the words are closed up and sealed until the time of the end" (Dan 12:9).

> For the revelation awaits an appointed time; it speaks of the end and will not prove false. Though it lingers, wait for it; it will certainly come and will not delay (Hab 2:3-4).

We should not assume that because we have been given a word that we have permission to share it. We must ask what the Holy Spirit wants us to do.

> *One of the lessons I have learned the hard way over the years is to not give a word prematurely. Often, the Lord will give a word well before the appointed time of release. This may be because intercessory prayer is necessary as part of the preparation, or it may be that it will take the hearer of the word a bit of time to get the whole word. And on occasion it is because the Lord wants the messenger of that word to grow into the reality of the word before it's released to others (Marc A Dupont).*

> *Prophets wait until they have received a word from the Lord, and they keep on waiting for proper timing (Lars Widerberg - The Seer).*

*There is no prophecy, which is not linked with tears, for the future is nearly always heavy with nameless terror (Nigg).*

## Four Principles

Four principles apply to the delivery of prophetic words

1. Ask the Lord how he wants the word delivered. If he is able to deliver a prophetic word, he is also able to give instructions about how he wants it delivered. Getting the delivery instructions right is just as important as getting the word right.

2. The speaker's only responsibility is to deliver the word in the way that he guides. Prophetic people are not accountable for the success or failure of the word, or the distance it travels.

3. The Holy Spirit is responsible for watching over his word and ensuring that it gets to those who need to hear it. He can achieve that in a multitude of ways. If a word is pure and clear, he can get it to those who need to hear it. He is an expert at getting the words cried in the wilderness into the throne room of the king.

4. Communicate clearly and precisely. The first task of the prophet is to listen to the Lord and get the word clear. A confused or impure word will go nowhere.

## Power of the Spirit

A prophetic word must be spoken in the power of the Spirit. A word that is not anointed by the Holy Spirit will fall flat and may be wasted, even if it is true.

> In the last days, God says, I will pour out my Spirit on all people. Your sons and daughters will prophesy, your young men will see visions, your old men will dream dreams. Even on my servants, both men and women, I will pour out my Spirit in those days, and they will prophesy (Acts 2:17-18).

*The prophet stood before men as a man who had been to stand before God (J A Motyer-Prophets and Prophecy).*

## Speak Boldly

Prophets should always speak boldly. They should avoid the temptation to soften God's word. They must make certain it is heard clearly.

> *Those who have messages from God must not be afraid of the faces of men (Matthew Henry).*

## Speak Clearly

A prophet should speak simply and clearly. There is no benefit in using King James English. An unclear word is a dead word. Joseph spoke clearly to Pharaoh.

> Seven years of great abundance are coming throughout the land of Egypt, but seven years of famine will follow them (Gen 41:29-30).

Joseph was accepted by Pharaoh, because he had received a clear straightforward message from the Holy Spirit. Daniel spoke clearly to King Belshazzar,

> This is what these words mean: God has numbered the days of your reign and brought it to an end. You have been weighed on the scales and found wanting. Your kingdom is divided and given to the Medes and Persians (Dan 5:26-28).

The Spirit gave him words that a king could understand.

God wants his prophets to speak to political and business leaders. They will only listen, if the prophets bring clear words. If prophets bring confusion and mystery, they will be ignored. Prophets must learn to hear what the Spirit is saying to the political and business leaders.

> *The best speakers for God are frequently they who are least gifted with human eloquence; for if that be richly present the mighty power of moving men—there is an imminent peril of relying on it, and attributing the results to its magnetic spell. God cannot give his glory to another. He may not share his praise with man (F B Meyer - Jeremiah).*

> *True prophets leave nothing to speculation, as their speech is precise and sometimes very blunt (Kingsley A Fletcher - The True Prophet in the Local Church).*

## Precise Prophecies

Prophets do not enjoy being shown up. A fear of being proved wrong can affect the presentation of prophecies. Two common ways are:

- Vague prophecies with precise timing
- Precise prophecies with vague timing.

The problem with these types of words is that no one will ever know if they have been fulfilled, so God is not honoured. On the other hand, they can never be proved wrong. Giving dates is not necessary, but listeners need to know, if the word is for the next few months (urgent), the next few years (get prepared), or later in the century (hope for long-term victory).

Jesus message in Matthew 24 is a wonderful example of a clear precise prophecy. He explained,

- What would happen;
- Why;
- When, with signs,
- Instructions.

Jesus was very clear about what would happen. The walls of the temple would be smashed and destroyed. This prophecy was fulfilled.

Jesus explained clearly why these events would happen. They would be the consequence of the stuff described in the previous chapter.

When asked when these things would happen, he gave a very precise answer. They would not happen immediately, but they would come in the lifetime of most of the people listening.

Jesus gave good advice about what to do when the troubles started. Christians should flee to the mountains. Those who heeded were kept safe.

Jesus also gave a couple of signs that would show them when the time for action was close (Jerusalem surrounded by an army). He also warned them not to be deceived by wars, famines, earthquakes and false religions. These types of event are common in every age, so they are not a sign of anything, except that a people have lost the blessing of God.

When asked about the second coming, Jesus said two things. First he did not know when it would happen. Second, there would be no signs of the second coming. It would occur when life was going on as normal on earth, so most people including Christians will not be expecting it.

Jesus also explained that this lack of signs does not matter. He told several parables, which explain what they should do. "Get on with doing the job you are called to do, so you will be ready when Jesus returns".

This is all very clear and precise, and gave Jesus' listeners everything that they needed to know. Nothing is missing. No questions were left unanswered. But many Christians cannot accept Jesus' clear precise message and turn it into something confusing, with multiple fulfilments, so that they can get what they want.

- They ignore Jesus' statement that there will be signs for the second coming and try to find signs.
- They ignore Jesus' statement that he does not know the day and the hour, and claim that they can know the month and the year and the season.
- They ignore Jesus' explanation that famines, earthquakes and wars are common in every unrighteous generation, and turn them into the true signs of the second coming.

No wonder many Christians are confused. The church has been crippled by too much prophetic mush. Every prophet should be aiming for clear precise prophecy.

## Spontaneous v Deliberate

Precision is an important value for prophetic people, because truth is important and there has been too much prophetic ambiguity masquerading as prophetic truth. The modern church tends to assume that spontaneous prophecy is more accurate. This is a crossover from the gift of prophecy, where spontaneity is the norm. However, there is no reason why spontaneous prophecy is superior to one that is pondered, and edited to sharpen the delivery of the message.

The Holy Spirit can do both spontaneous and deliberate, and he is free to choose how he will operate in any situation. To shake us out of our comfort zones, he will sometimes be spontaneous, when we want to be deliberate, and he will often be more deliberate, when we want to be spontaneous.

The benefit of a spontaneous word is that the Holy Spirit can drop it into our hearts unexpectedly, before our minds wind up, and before the flesh starts getting in the way. This is fine for beginners, but it not the basis for developing into a prophetic ministry. The person who wants to be used by God in prophecy must learn to quiet their mind and distinguish their own thoughts from the voice of the Spirit. This is difficult and takes time, but is essential for developing a prophetic gifting. Relying on the Holy Spirit to beat our minds with spontaneous words is not a long-term solution.

The Holy Spirit loves to surprise us, so he will continue to give us words when we are not expecting anything, but clinging to the spontaneous will keep us locked in immaturity. Those who want to be used in prophecy will have to work hard at learning to calm their minds deliberately and carefully seek the words of the Lord. Sometimes precision is worth waiting for.

> Pearls take time to polish:
> Mush tends to gush in a flush.

"Rapid fire" prophecy is not superior to a measured word.

Many prophecies would be clearer, if they were reviewed and edited by the prophet or other prophetic people. Many prophecies are spot on for the first few sentences, but then the speaker loses their way towards the end. Someone should probably have put the editor's pencil through the last few sentences.

## Mixing Prophecy and Application

A prophecy and its application must not be confused. The application of a prophecy can be unclear, especially if it is intended for a different person or a different time, or the listeners have hard hearts. The prophecy itself should be clear and precise.

This principle is evident from the scriptures. The application of many prophecies is unclear. Often the application is not clear until they have been fulfilled. This is true of Revelation. Much of the application of John's vision will not be clear until the time when it is fulfilled.

The prophetic word itself is always very clear and precise. The prophets did not just dictate what they heard the Holy Spirit saying like automatons. They received a revelation from God and wrote down or spoke what they had received. Their words were carefully honed. Much of Jeremiah's prophecy is presented as poetry. John recorded the revelations he received on Patmos with an amazing economy of words, yet what he saw is vividly and precisely described.

Jesus never rambled. The beatitudes are amazingly precise and clear. Their application was much more difficult. Jesus could tell a complicated parable in just a few words, because his communication was precise and clear. His listeners understood the story, but often missed the application.

Isaiah 53 is a good example. The application of this prophecy was unclear until Jesus had died on the cross. However, the prophecy itself was very clear and precise.

Reading it now, it is obvious that every word was important and is exactly where the Holy Spirit wanted it to be.

The biblical prophets were very precise when writing and speaking their words. They knew they would quite likely be misunderstood by a people with hardened hearts, so they made sure that they did not give them an excuse, by speaking vaguely.

The application of a prophecy will often be unclear. People with hardened hearts will just not get it, but that is not an excuse for prophets to be lazy with their presentation. Much modern prophecy is ignored, because the wording is just too sloppy.

## Prophetic Timing

The timing of prophecy is important. There are two situations with regard to timing in the prophetic scriptures.

1) Some prophecies are conditional, so there is no time attached to them.

2) In other prophecies, God is very precise about timing.

Christian prophets need to do better with the timing of their words. When a revelation comes, the prophetic should ask four questions.

1) When is the revelation to be communicated?

2) How is it to be communicated?

3) Is it conditional or does it have a specific timing?

4) What is the timing?

The fourth question depends on the answer to the third.

We have not received a full revelation until we have the answers to all these questions. Some people get so excited about receiving a revelation that they forget to press in for the rest. They stop before they have the lot.

## Seeing in Part

Seeing in part is not as an excuse for mediocre prophecy.

> For we know in part and we prophesy in part, but when completeness comes, what is in part disappears…..For now we see only a reflection as in a mirror; then we shall see face to face. Now I know in part; then I shall know fully, even as I am fully known (1 Cor 13:9-12).

Paul is explaining our human situation, not providing an excuse for weak prophecy. We see in part, because God cannot reveal his full glory to his people on earth.

The common saying that we always see through a "dark glass". That is not what Paul was saying. He is actually explaining the difference between our situation now and that in the next life. Because we live in the physical world, we miss most of what is happening in the spiritual world. Human minds just cannot comprehend the reality of the new heaven and new earth.

## Vision and Context

God speaks into the context of our experience. He mostly uses the images, words and places with which we are familiar. When prophets communicate their messages, they should use words and images that are familiar to their listeners.

Sometimes God gives a seer a vision that goes beyond familiar words and images. The seer has to translate what he saw using the words and images with which he was familiar. John's Revelation is a good example of this. Here is a description of something he saw.

> At once I was in the Spirit, and there before me was a throne in heaven with someone sitting on it. And the one who sat there had the appearance of jasper and ruby. A rainbow that shone like an emerald encircled the throne (Rev 4:2-3).

I doubt that John saw jaspars, rubies and emeralds. These are physical things and John had been given a glimpse into the spiritual world. He saw things that were beyond his earthly experience, so he was trying to describe the indescribable. He used images of the most beautiful things on earth to describe the wonder of the spiritual world, but this is just a hint of its glory.

The biblical prophets used everyday language and context to describe what they saw, but they were also very clear about what was a revelation from God and what was a description of their response to their experience.

## Sharing Visions

The Holy Spirit often shows the prophet an image or a vision. This is just another way of communicating. God uses images just to strengthen the power of communication, because audio-visual communication can be more effective that written words.

God does not speak in images just to suit the learning style of the seer, but for the benefit of all his people. The images received are not the property of the seer.

If a Christian has been shown images by the Holy Spirit, the vision should be recorded as accurately as possible. This is what the biblical prophets did. Daniel and John described what they saw (sometimes not very well, because human language was not up to it).

The Christian should pray about whether and when to share the vision. Often the Lord does not give permission to share until long after the vision is received. Receiving a vision does not constitute permission to publish it.

Once consent to share has been given, the vision should be described as accurately as possible. The best practice is to describe what was seen "I saw....." Any contextual information or interpretation should be presented separately. "I believe this means…" This approach has several benefits.

1) Other Christians can test the seer's seeing (Maybe he ate too much ketchup with his fries last night).

2) Listeners are encouraged to think about the nature of what the seer has seen,
   - something that will happen (1 Kings 22:17),
   - a symbol of a real entity (Daniel's beast), or
   - a symbolic presentation of a spiritual reality (Amos's lion hiding in the thicket).

   Seers often confuse these three different types of vision when interpreting what they have seen.

3) Other people can then apply what the seer has seen to their situation. It may be different from the seer's.

4) Listeners are free to decide about the timing of the fulfilment, if it is not contained in the vision.

5) Other people can test the interpretation of the vision. Sometimes another person will provide a better interpretation of a dream and vision than the seer. Daniel understood the meaning of Nebuchadnezzar's dream better than he did. Some seers are not gifted at interpretation of visions.

Distinguishing what the Sprit is showing from what the person already knows is difficult, but is really important. We have the same difficulty in distinguishing the voice of the Spirit from thoughts that pop out of our minds. Learning to distinguish the two is critical for sharpening the prophetic gifting. Unfortunately many prophets do not bother trying.

If the seer has struggled to distinguish the two, there is nothing wrong with saying that to the readers. Being humble does not diminish a gifting. The Holy Spirit is capable of highlighting what he wants people to see or hear.

**Recording Dreams and Visions**
A vision should be written down as soon as it is received. If too much time passes, extraneous stuff can creep in as the memory dims.

When recording dreams and visions, the details of the dream or vision must be kept separate from the interpretation. If the Lord gave some interpretation during the dream, then that should be spelt out clearly too. The person who had the dream or vision knows what they saw, so there should not be any debate about the content. However, there can be debate about whether the dream came from God, or the forces of evil, or was just the working of the dreamers mind. Dreams and visions should be tested by the body of Christ.

Unless the Holy Spirit gives a specific interpretation and application during the dream or vision, the interpretation of a dream or vision can be open to debate. Sometimes the person who receives the dream or vision may not be the best person to provide interpretation. Joseph and Daniel were prophetic people who were skilled in interpreting dreams.

The best practice is to record the dream and vision as accurately as possible, and then give the interpretation separately. This was Daniels approach in Daniel 7 and 8. In the first part of each chapter he describes what he saw. He then gives the interpretation that was given to him by the angel. He did not attempt to give his own interpretation.

The book of Revelation is similar. John recorded all that he saw very carefully and precisely. He rarely gives any interpretation (except that stars are angels, lampstands are churches, waters are people, heads are kings, hills are kings). I presume that the Holy Spirit did not give John the interpretation of his vision, so he did not try to give one.

Most Christians who have a dream or vision to share seem to feel bound to give the interpretation and application at the same time. Moreover, the content and the interpretation are often mixed up together, making it hard to assess the source of the dream. This also makes it hard to assess the interpretation. Likewise, if the dream or vision is not described clearly without interpretation, a person who is gifted in interpreting dreams and visions will find it difficult to give an alternative interpretation.

## Right Attitude

Prophecy must be delivered in the right attitude. We must speak the truth in love. A wrong attitude nullifies the truth of the word. Many true prophecies have been made false, because they have been spoken in a harsh or critical attitude.

All prophets should note God's response when he saw the sins of the people who lived during the time of Noah.

> The Lord was grieved that he had made man on the earth,
> and his heart was filled with pain (Gen 6:6).

God's heart was "filled with pain". A prophet cannot represent God during a time of judgement unless his heart is filled with pain.

## Right Spirit

Some Christians say, "A prophet's job is to say what God says". This is correct, but it is only part of the truth. A prophet's job is to say what God says in the right spirit. Many prophets have spoken a true word without it being heard. Sometimes the true word was not received because the listener's heart was hard, but more often it was not heard, because the spirit of the prophet was warped.

I remember a woman who was really upset, because her pastor had not received a word that she and a friend had given to him. She could not understand why this had happened, because the word was true. Her word rung true to me too, but I could tell from the tone of her voice why she was not heard. She oozed bitterness, hurt and frustration.

The hard truth for prophets to accept is that being correct is not enough. A true word from God can be nullified by a wrong spirit. In the spiritual dimension, a true word spoken wrongly is exactly the same as a false word. When God's heart is "filled with pain" (Gen 6:6), he cannot be represented by just the truth. Jeremiah was a powerful prophet, because he felt the pain on God's heart.

### Truth without love is not truth.

Most prophets put a lot of effort into hearing what God is saying, but few put the same effort into keeping their spirit right. A prophet can never just say, "I spoke God's truth, I have done my bit". Every prophet should be asking, "Did I speak God's word in God's way."

> *If you prophesy you need to root out every lie - every white lie, every effort to deceive or mislead, every half-truth—because if you do not get rid of them, the same spirit that gets into your tongue when you lie, will try to get hold of your tongue when you prophesy. If we speak the word of the Lord in prophecy we dare not allow room for less than the truth on any occasion (Ed Traut).*

## Giving Bad News

Delivering bad news to a person who has asked for a prophetic word is tricky for a prophetic person. The prophet must keep their heart right. Prophets who find it harder to give bad news than good news should ponder the reason. Maybe they think that if bad news does not eventuate, they will look mean, whereas if they give good news and it does not happen, the person will not mind. Unfortunately, giving good news that is not inspired by God can do serious harm to the person receiving it. Prophets should check carefully that they are right, whether they have good or bad news.

If God gives a prophet a word for someone, he can also explain how to give it. If he asks them to give bad news, they should ask him how he wants it presented.

- Micah used humour and hyperbole to give bad news to Ahab. Despite the funny way that Micah presented his word, Ahab got the message (1 Kings 22:15-23).

111

- Nathan told David a parable, which drew him into sympathy for the victim, making it difficult for him to reject the hard word (2 Sam 12:1-7).
- Jeremiah uses symbolic actions to bring bad news, and to give hope. This made people curious, which opened their hearts to the word (Jer 13:1-11).

Asking God how to give a hard word is very important. Whether bringing good news or bad news, the prophet should present it in a humble way. It does not hurt to say, "This is not nice, but it is what I got from the Lord. You are welcome to test it".

Love is most important of all. If people know that we love them, they will find it easier to accept bad news from us.

**Courtesy**

If a prophecy is for a church, the prophet should find out who God wants it delivered to. Delivering the word to the congregation is wrong, if God intends it to be delivered to the elders and pastors. Prophets should be courteous and abide by the protocols that prevail in that particular church.

Perceptions about the one who brings the word inevitably have a bearing on the attitude to the word. Prophetic people resent this, but it is the truth. The church is entitled to judge prophets by the fruit of the spirit in their lives.

**The Word belongs to God**

Once the word is delivered, the prophet's task is finished; apart from prayer. Prophets must leave the results to God. A prophet, who nags in support of a word, quickly loses credibility and detracts from the Word. God does not nag. Deliver the word in the right way, in the right attitude and God will do the rest. Luke 14:7-10 is relevant to sharing prophecy and vision.

> When he noticed how the guests picked the places of honor at the table, Jesus told them this parable: When someone invites you to a wedding feast, do not take the place of honor, for a person more distinguished than you may have been invited. If so, the host who invited both of you will come and say to you, 'Give this person your seat.' Then, humiliated, you will have to take the least important place. But when you are invited, take the lowest place, so that when your host comes, he will say to you, 'Friend, move up to a better place.' Then you will be honored in the presence of all the other guests.

Prophetic people are often tempted to find a higher place at the banquet for their words and visions. They do this in various ways.

- Turning the text into the first person.
- Using King James English
- Adding proof texts
- Quoting big name prophets
- Getting them onto the best prophetic lists.
- Adding dramatic graphics
- Playing sombre music in the background.

The authority of the prophetic comes from the witness of the Spirit in the heart of the hearer.

We should present our words and visions in a humble way near the bottom of the table. Then the Holy Spirit can move them up to the top of the table, if he wishes. This does not mean that we should put our words under the table with the dogs. We do not need to grovel.

# 8

# Prophets and Intercessors

Intercessors pray:
- They release the Holy Spirit and the angels to do the Fathers will on earth.
- They stand together to resist the attacks of the enemy on behalf of a church, a city or a nation.

Prophets speak:
- They explain God's purpose for churches, cities and nations to his people.
- Some warn God's people of danger and explain how they should respond to it.
- A few speak to the world and warn of judgment and describe how it can be averted (Jonah and Nineveh).

Intercessors and Prophets will sometimes receive a revelation of coming disasters, but the purpose will be different.

## Revelation to Prophets

Prophets will sometimes receive a revelation of a future disaster.
- They are called to speak to God's people and explain how God wants them to respond during the crisis. Following this guidance will lead to blessing.

- o In some situations, they might need to flee to survive.
- o In other situations, God will want them to stand their ground and suffer in the face of evil.

- A few prophets will be called to speak to a city or nation and warn of danger that is coming as a consequence of sin. When they do this, they should also call the city or nation to repentance. They must give guidance to God's people about how they should respond.

- The revelations received by prophets will mostly be conditional. If the city or nation responds appropriately, the event will be held back. The conditions for this should be clearly specified.

- Prophets should not speak out words about the future, just to show that God is clever. He does not play that game.

- Prophets speak with purpose. Without guidance, conditions or a challenge, a prophet is just a clanging gong.

- When prophets receive a revelation of trouble in the future, they should not speak immediately, but test the word with other people they trust.

- The prophet should also pray about when, how and to whom the word should be spoken. They should pray about what God wants his people to do and how he wants the city or nation to respond. Without these things, the prophetic word is not complete.

- God shows prophets things that will happen and explains what the people should do.

- For prophets, explaining what people must do is as important as warning of what will happen.

## Revelation to Intercessors

God often reveals the plans of the enemy to intercessors, so they can stand against them in the Spirit and prevent the evil from occurring.

- God is showing them something that will not happen, if they are doing their job.
- These revelations can be scary, so intercession is not for the fainthearted.
- Intercessors should guard their revelations carefully and not hand them around casually (Matt 7:6).
- Intercessors should share and test their revelations with other intercessors who are strong enough to handle the revelation.
- When these revelations are circulated widely among Christians, they create confusion within the church. Even if the intercessors do their job and prevent the event from taking place, the enemy can use them to inspire fear.
- A revelation given to inspire intercession has several characteristics that can be confusing to Christians.
  - They usually do not take place, so Christians assume the revelation was wrong, without understanding that it was not fulfilled, because the intercessors did their job.
  - They are sometimes symbolic. Ezekiel saw the sun, moon and stars going dark. This was not fulfilled literally, but was a description of Egypt's Pharaohs being defeated by the Emperor of Babylon (Ezekiel 32:7). Intercessors need to be skilled in interpreting these symbolic messages.
  - Intercessors are often called to pray against evil attacks that God does not want to happen. In this situation, the revelation they receive, will not include a call to repentance, or specify conditions that must be met to prevent its fulfilment, as that is not the reason why it was given.

- o God does not give guidance about how to live through the evil events he reveals to intercessors, because he does not intend them to happen. When these revelations get into the hands of other Christians, they get confused, because they do not know what to do. The revelation is there with nothing around it.
- o Most of the revelations received by intercessors will be things that God wants to do. They will happen if the intercessors pray seriously. Intercessors will need to be skilled in discerning between things that God wants to accomplish and the plans of the enemy that he wants thwarted.

## Merged Roles

The role of prophet and intercessor sometimes merges in one person. When this happens, the person should be very clear about what they are doing. When they receive a revelation about the future, they should seek guidance from God about whether it is for the prayer closet or the prophetic platform. They should also clarify whether it is something God wants to do or a plan of the enemy that he wants to foil.

## Clear Voice

The absence of a prophetic voice in a city creates uncertainty about the cause of traumatic events and their spiritual significance. Most of the commentary on disasters usually comes from pastors whose focus is on providing care for people who have lost homes or family members. Their main goal is to put guilt and guidance out of scope, so they leave God's purposes out of the situation. Unfortunately, many other Christians find this explanation inadequate and are uncertain about how they should respond to these events. They see Jesus applying spiritual significance to physical disasters (Luke 13:1-5) and want the same for their time.

Without a clear trumpet call, the people go and look for their own answers. They get muddled and grab what they can. Revelations that God has given to intercessors can begin to circulate as prophecies about the future. This creates confusion, because the revelations contain no guidance to Christians about how to respond. There is no call to repentance for the people of the world or condition that must be met to avert the disaster. This is not surprising, because that was not their purpose.

The intercessors should focus on doing their job by standing in prayer against the plans of the enemy that God has revealed to them. If the intercessors are fulfilling their calling, these events will not take place. God has revealed these things to the intercessors, because he does not want them to happen.

The thirst for revelation that emerges during a crisis cannot be quenched by the revelations received by intercessors.

> Where there is no revelation, the people are left naked (Prov 29:18).

Unfortunately, scraps from tables of the intercessors will not satisfy this hunger for revelation.

The problem is lack of revelation. We should be praying that God will release a clear prophetic voice that we may have better understanding of God's purposes. If God is giving warnings about events that are going to happen, the prophets should be listening and seeking guidance about his plans for his people and asking what changes must take place to avert the disaster.

# 9

# Prophetic Pitfalls

God cares about the character of the prophet as much as for the truth of their words. There are several pitfalls, which prophets, young and old, must be careful to avoid.

## a) A Critical and Harsh Spirit

Prophets have high standards. They see things in black and white. This can sometimes result in the prophet being over critical, which makes their words seem harsh, even if they are true. A prophet who enjoys giving hard words may have a critical spirit. The downside of a prophetic calling is a propensity to judge others, especially in the areas of our own weaknesses.

## b) Frustration and Bitterness

All prophets experience rejection, if their words are not accepted and obeyed. If this happens frequently, the prophet can become frustrated, which often leads to bitterness. Words spoken out of frustration and bitterness will be contaminated and not come out pure. This is one of the most serious problems faced by prophets. They must learn to deal with rejection without going into frustration and bitterness.

*Frustration is an enemy to the prophetic ministry. It will always colour our thinking, infect the word we have, and give us a jaundiced perspective on the life of the church. If we are to represent God's heart and be good servants, we must learn to master our frustration (Graham Cooke - Developing Your Prophetic Gifting).*

*Prophetic people are especially susceptible to rejection. This rejection can lead to bitterness, negativism, and self-pity – all things that make prophetic people useless for the ministry of the Holy Spirit (Jack Deere Surprised - By the Voice of God).*

*A cave seems to be a safe place, but it is not a dwelling place. The Body of Christ is full of wounded prophets who went into a cave and dwelt there (Janet Chambers - Cave Dweller or Tower Dweller).*

## c) Rejoicing in Rejection

Prophetic people often take rejection of their words as a sign that they were true. This is dangerous, because it can hide problems. Rejection often occurs because the word was not clear, or was spoken in the wrong spirit.

Prophets must be constantly looking at the way they present their message. They should hone their words, so they can present a clearer message. Praise from friends and people who have received the word does not mean much. We are all receptive to words that confirm our own views. The real test of a word is whether it is clear to those who are challenged by it.

## d) Prophetic Pushiness

Prophets must avoid the trap of pushing their name forward. This pushiness often comes from frequent rejection, but it must be rejected. Prophets must be servants of God's word. Their only concern is for the word to be received. If the word is heard, it does not matter if the prophet is forgotten. Prophets are human, so this is easier to say than to live. When prophets hear a word they have received being quoted without their name being mentioned, their heart screams for attention. This feeling is human, but is dangerous for the prophet, because it is rooted in pride, and pride kills prophecy. Prophets must struggle to quiet their hearts and be content if the word they spoke is being heard.

## e) Misuse of Power

Prophets must not use their authority to harm people. Elijah misused his gifting by speaking a curse that released two bears to kill the rude children (2 Kings 2:23-25). The scriptures do not say that Elijah's behaviour was correct. They just record the incident. Elijah was not perfect, he just did his best with the knowledge that he had. With our knowledge of Jesus and his teaching, it is clear that Elijah misused his gifting. The boys who mocked him were irrelevant. He should have just ignored them.

James and John were misusing prophetic power when they tried to call down fire from heaven on those who opposed them. Jesus warned that they were acting in the wrong spirit. Prophets must not use their gifting to protect their role or their reputation.

## f) Pride

Prophets usually lead lives that are extremely righteous. They can easily take on the spirit of the Pharisees, who felt good, because they could see the sins of other people. Pride can destroy a prophetic ministry.

The arrogant cannot stand in your presence (Psalm 5:5).

## g) Rationalising Mistakes

Some prophets are so worried about being wrong that they refuse to admit mistakes. No prophet is always right.

*Sometimes a prophetic person has a hard time admitting a mistake because he or she thinks it would ruin their credibility. Usually just the opposite happens. Rationalising or failing to admit our mistakes is what usually ruins credibility. People trust people who say they were wrong (Jack Deere - Surprised by the Voice of God).*

## h) Control and Manipulation

The Jezebel spirit uses manipulation and control to achieve results (1 Kings 21:7-11). It is the opposite and the enemy of the prophetic. Prophets must avoid all temptation to "help" the fulfilment of their words by manipulating people.

## i) Rebellion

Pride often leads to rebellion. Rebellion is crippling for a prophet, as it is the moral equivalent of witchcraft (1 Sam 15:23).

## j) Jealousy

Prophets can often become jealous of other ministries that seem to receive much more honour and acceptance. Jealousy can prevent us from hearing clearly.

## k) People Pleasing

People pleasing is a killer for all ministry, and especially the prophetic. Prophetic people who tell people what they want to hear will lose touch with God (Gal 1:10; Ezek 13:2). A true prophet should not expect the praise of people (Luke 6:26), they will seek only the approval of God.

> *Human love can taint a word. Sometimes love blinds the prophet, causing him or her to give a good prophetic word when the Lord wanted to give a word of correction (Cindy Jacobs - The Voice of God).*

## l) Calling Out Sins Publicly

Prophets should not publicly accuse individuals of sin. The gospel provides guidelines for dealing with Christians who sin. They should first be spoken to in private.

> If your brother sins against you, go and show him his fault, just between the two of you. If he listens to you, you have won your brother over. But if he will not listen, take one or two others along, so that 'every matter may be established by the testimony of two or three witnesses.' If he refuses to listen to them, tell it to the church; and if he refuses to listen even to the church, treat him as you would a pagan or a tax collector (Matthew 18:15-17).

124

## m) Blindness to the Culture

The hardest thing for a prophet to see is the weakness and sins of their own society, culture or denomination. If we are attached to something, we can be blinded by it. A true prophet stands apart from their culture.

## n) Money

Money can be a cause of blindness. Prophets should be careful about giving favourable words to those who provide them with financial support. Prophets should try to be financially independent of their church and community.

> *Materialism and money have always been a problem in prophetic ministry. Micah complained in his day, "This is what the Lord says: 'As for the prophets who lead my people astray, if one feeds them, they proclaim 'peace'; if he does not, they prepare to wage war against him" (Mic 3:5).*

> *When prophets succumb to the temptation to give good prophecies to those who treat them well and bad prophecies to those who don't show them special deference, then the Lord may cease speaking to any of the prophetic people (Jack Deere Surprised By the Voice of God).*

## o) Sexual Immorality

Prophets must be very careful about sexual temptation.

> *Any ministry can fall prey to any sin, but prophetic people seem to be especially prone to sexual sin. Perhaps one reason is because of the heightened sensitivity that comes with the prophetic gift. While prophetic individuals can "feel" the movement of the Holy Spirit, but they can also feel the torment of demonic spirits that attack them through others (John Paul Jackson).*

## p) Confusing Wisdom and Prophecy

A prophet must distinguish between what they receive from the Lord and what comes from their own wisdom. Those who are unable to make the distinction are on a very slippery slope, which often leads to words from the Lord being lost among "prophetic babble". If the prophet is not sure, it is better to be modest than to exalt their wisdom.

# 10

# Testing Prophets

We should welcome prophecies, but they should always be tested.

> Do not put out the Spirit's fire; do not treat prophecies with contempt. Test everything. Hold on to the good. Avoid every kind of evil (1 Thes 5:19-22).

## Living with Imperfection

No prophets are perfect. Even experienced prophets will get it wrong sometimes. I suspect that most prophets would be very happy, if they got it right 90 percent of the time. Many prophecies that are from God will be slightly contaminated by something that has been added from the prophet's heart. This is normal even for experienced prophets, because all prophets are human.

The solution is not to reject prophecy, but to test everything. Even if a word comes from a "big name" prophet, we should not assume that it is correct. Christians can feel guilty about rejecting a word that came from a well-known prophet, but no prophet can guarantee a perfect word. The pressure on famous speakers may make them prone to more frequent mistakes.

God allows his prophets to make mistakes to keep them humble and to prevent the church from becoming too dependent on them. We must become more relaxed and comfortable in dealing with impure and incorrect prophecies, so that they can be discarded without drama. As we get better at testing prophecies, we will get better at calmly saying, "That was not from God" or "He missed the bus".

We must also learn to reject prophecies without killing the prophet. The church should accept a mistake as a reminder that all prophets are human. Prophets should be glad to hear about their mistakes, so they can learn from them.

> *Prophets must humbly accept the truth that they see through a glass darkly, that they know only in part. In other words, they make mistakes. Mature prophets urge everyone to who they prophesy to judge, test and compare with scripture everything they say. They are not offended when people are careful (Stephen L Mansfield - Pastoring the Prophetic).*

## Testing prophecies

The Bible gives a number of principles for testing a prophecy.

- 1 Cor 14:4      - builds up the body,
- 2 Tim 3:16      - agrees with Scripture,
- John 16:13-14      - exalts Jesus,
- Deut 18:22      - comes true.
- Deut 13:1-5      - leads to God and obedience to him,
- Rom 8:15      - produces liberty,
- 2 Cor 3:6      - produces life,
- 1 John 2:27      - attested to the Holy Spirit.

All prophecies should glorify and honour Jesus.

> At this I fell at his feet to worship him. But he said to me, "Do not do it! I am a fellow servant with you and with your brothers who hold to the testimony of Jesus. Worship God! For the testimony of Jesus is the spirit of prophecy" (Rev 19:10).

Sometimes it is hard to test a prophecy. A word may seem to be okay, but it may take time before it is fulfilled. Some words of encouragement are consistent with scripture and hard to prove wrong. In these situations, testing of prophets may be more helpful.

## Reliable Prophets

Every church needs a prophet who has a proven track record, a person who is known for speaking the word of the Lord. It is often easier to test prophets than individual prophecies. A prophet can be watched over time to see if their life is bearing fruit for the Lord (Matthew 7:15-20). Every church needs a proven prophet who can be trusted to bring a reliable word when one is required.

The restoration of the prophetic ministry is one of the most urgent needs of the modern church. The danger in times of need is that God's people will accept second best. We must not accept every person who claims to be a prophet, but test them to discover those that are sent by the Lord. If the church is to release prophets into their full ministry, it must learn to recognise those who are truly called.

Jesus warned that false prophets and deceivers would come upon the earth, and that even some of the elect would be deceived by them (Mark 13:22-23). False prophets have been present in the world in every age, but they are particularly common in times of tumult.

In our time, we have seen a great outburst of prophetic activity with all kinds of individuals and cults claiming to have the truth. In this situation, the church not only needs prophets who speak God's truth, but must learn to discern the true from the false. Whenever God releases a particular gift in the world, Satan tries to release a counterfeit of that gift. We can be sure that as God restores the prophetic ministry, Satan will try to raise up false prophets.

The Bible gives a number of tests for discerning true prophets from those who are false. All Christians should be familiar with them.

## a) Calling

A true prophetic ministry always begins with a call from God (Jer 1:4-10; Is 6:1-8). The initiative in the making of a prophet always rests with him, not the person being called. Jeremiah condemned the false prophets because they had not stood in the presence of the Lord to hear his voice. They could not speak his word because they had not heard him speak (Jer 23:18,22). The true prophetic ministry always begins with the call of God.

## b) Fulfilled Words

Moses made an important statement about testing prophets.

> If what a prophet proclaims in the name of the Lord does not take place or come true that is a message the Lord has not spoken. That prophet has spoken presumptuously (Deut 18:22).

If the word of a prophet is not fulfilled, then they may be a false prophet. This test must be used with care. Sometimes a word is not fulfilled, because the people repent or God shows mercy and postpones judgement. The test applies more to positive prophecies.

The proof that a prophet has been called is words that are effective and fulfilled. A good example of this was Samuel.

> The Lord was with Samuel as he grew up, and he let none of his words fall to the ground. And all Israel from Dan to Beersheba recognised that Samuel was attested as a prophet (1 Sam 3:19-20).

The fact that his words were fulfilled showed that God was with him and was proof of his call. A true prophet will be recognised by other Christians.

> *If God is able to find the right vessel the Word will come forth in abundance (Chip Brogden - Letter to a Reluctant Prophet).*

## c) False Gods

Prophets who encourage people to worship false gods are not true prophets. Even if they perform signs and wonders they should not be followed. They are false prophets.

> If a prophet, or one who foretells by dreams, appears among you and announces for you a miraculous sign or wonder, and if the sign or wonder of which he has spoken takes place, and he says, "Let us follow other gods,"....you must not listen to the words of that prophet or dreamer. The Lord your God is testing you to find out whether you love him with all your heart and with all your soul (Deut 13:1-3).

Jesus is the one who inspires and fulfils all prophecy (Rev 19:10). All prophecy should be centred on him.

## d) Character

Character is one of the best tests of a prophet. Jesus said,

> Watch out for false prophets. They come to you in sheep's clothing, but inwardly they are ferocious wolves. By their fruit you will recognise them (Matt 7:15-16).

He went on to say that a bad tree cannot bear good fruit. A person who is not living a holy life should not be acknowledged as a prophet. True prophets will demonstrate the fruit of the spirit in their daily lives.

## e) Theology

When John was writing about discerning truth from error, he said that a true spirit will acknowledge that Jesus has come in the flesh (1 John 4:2). This is a theological test. A true prophet will have a correct understanding of the truth about Jesus. People who teach strange things about him are likely to be false prophets.

## f) Discernment

Every fellowship needs people who are experienced with the gift of discernment. They should be able to discern the false prophet from true prophet.

# 11

# False Prophets

Whenever God revives a ministry, Satan brings forth a counterfeit. That should not put us off, just make us careful. If we hear that counterfeit money is in circulation, we do not stop using money. We just become more careful. As the prophetic ministry grows, false prophets will become more prevalent. We should not reject prophecy, but be vigilant. Elders should guard against false prophets by allowing a fully developed ministry to emerge in their church. True prophets are the best antidote to false prophets.

Jesus warned that false prophets would come as wolves dressed in sheep's clothing

> Watch out for false prophets. They come to you in sheep's clothing, but inwardly they are ferocious wolves. By their fruit you will recognise them. Do people pick grapes from thornbushes, or figs from thistles? Likewise every good tree bears good fruit, but a bad tree bears bad fruit. A good tree cannot bear bad fruit, and a bad tree cannot bear good fruit. Every tree that does not bear good fruit is cut down and thrown into the fire. Thus, by their fruit you will recognise them (Matt 7:15-20).

False prophets are not always obvious. They appear to be credible, but can do incredible damage to the flock.

The Bible has strong warnings for false prophets (Ezek 13:1-12; Jer 5:12-13; Jer 6:13-15; Jer 23:15-18).

> But there were also false prophets among the people, just as there will be false teachers among you. They will secretly introduce destructive heresies, even denying the sovereign Lord who bought them—bringing swift destruction on themselves. Many will follow their shameful ways and will bring the way of truth into disrepute. In their greed these teachers will exploit you with stories they have made up. Their condemnation has long been hanging over them, and their destruction has not been sleeping (2 Pet 2:1-3).

## Court Prophets

In Old Testament times the most serious problem was the "court prophets", who were part of the establishment and acted as cheerleaders for their king, whether he was obeying God or doing evil (1 Kings 22). The modern equivalent is the "pet prophet" who "barks on command" for a pastor-leader. Prophets must not join the establishment.

> I did not send these prophets, yet they have run with their message; I did not speak to them, yet they have prophesied. But if they had stood in my council, they would have proclaimed my words to my people and would have turned them from their evil ways and from their evil deeds (Jer 23:21-22).

## Platform Prophets

The root problem with one-man leadership is that those who get to the top often feel insecure, so they surround themselves with "Yes Men". Anyone who might challenge their authority is kept at a distance. The other side of this problem is the platform or pedestal prophet. The senior pastor who does not have his own "pet prophet" brings one in from outside and puts him on a pedestal. The platform prophet is allowed to give encouragement to the people and challenge those that need sorting out, but the senior pastor always stands behind the prophet on the platform, safe from challenging words.

This is an unhealthy relationship. The platform prophet has authority because the senior pastor testifies to his credibility. In return for this authentication, the platform prophet must submit to the authority of the pastor-manager and honour him. The prophet is kept on the pedestal where their ministry can be controlled. The platform prophet must go along with this charade, or be kept in silence.

## End-times Industry
The most serious form of false prophecy in the modern church is the "end-times" industry. Their teaching that,

- the world will get worse,
- Jesus is returning soon,
- the kingdom will not be established soon,
- America is God's servant to control the world,

has been Satan's best scheme for crippling the church. Although these prophet's "dates" and predictions have been wrong again and again, they are still accepted by the church. They were wrong about Y2K, but they never apologised. We live in a gullible age. Christians should be careful about following teachers who have persisted in being wrong.

## Comfort Prophets
Prophets who only give positive messages are dangerous. There are too many comfort prophecies and not enough prophecies that have come out of the council of God.

> Give us no more visions of what is right! Tell us pleasant things, prophesy illusions. Leave this way, get off this path, and stop confronting us with the Holy One of Israel! (Is 30:10-11).

> But the prophet who prophesies peace will be recognised as one truly sent by the Lord only if prediction comes true (Jer 28:9).

Man prophets of revival assume that the church can have revival without changing. They assume that God will reward lethargy and lukewarmness with revival and blessing.

## Internet Prophets

With the advance of the internet, a terrific flood of prophecies has flowed out to the Christian community. Unfortunately, much of what is shared is poor quality. This is a serious problem for the church and could seriously damage the credibility of the prophetic ministry. The internet has been a marvellous vehicle for the distribution of prophecy, but unless there is more testing of these prophecies, God's people will be swamped with chaff and begin to "despise prophecy".

## Calendars and Codes

A prophetic distraction that has emerged among Christians in recent years is using the numbers of the years in the Hebrew calendar to explain what God is going to do in the world. The problem is that the Holy Spirit inspired the scriptures, but he has not inspired a calendar. There is no guarantee that the Hebrew calendar has numbered the years since Adam's birth correctly. That does not matter for those who want to obey God, but it becomes a problem, if we want to use dates in either the Gregorian or Hebrew calendar to predict the future. The dates are just too uncertain for much significance to be placed on them.

The Holy Spirit can speak clearly. Christian prophets should focus on learning to hear the Holy Spirit speak. Looking for signs in dates and shadows is pointless effort.

The Bible code is another prophetic distraction. A series of messages supposedly contained within the Bible text are decoded into words and phrases that demonstrate foreknowledge and prophecy. The Bible Code is a pointless exercise. Even if Hitler's name is hidden somewhere in the Hebrew Torah, it does not help me to be a better Christian. I would prefer ten clear words spoken by the Holy Spirit to a thousand from a Bible code.

## Israel determines History of the Church

In recent years a strange doctrine has emerged. Many Bible teachers believe that what happens in the church is determined by events in the nation of Israel. They urge Christians to watch what happens in Israel to understand what is happening in the church. This is a false teaching.

Firstly, what happens in the church is determined by the Holy Spirit. He is not constrained by political or national leaders in any nation. The only thing that constrains his work is the unwillingness of Christians to follow him. We can hold back his activity by refusing to trust and obey him.

Secondly, the leaders of the nation of Israel are not Christians. They have refused to acknowledge Jesus as their Messiah. They do not walk in the Spirit, so they do not hear his voice. Many do not acknowledge God or honour his law. The leaders of Israel continue to disobey the law, so they are living outside the blessing of the covenant. A nation in this state cannot control the Holy Spirit's work on earth.

The reverse is true. What happens on earth is largely determined by the church. When the church is weak, the world goes downhill. When the church is led by the Holy Spirit and walks in his power, the world is transformed.

Many Christians see the restoration of Israel is a marker for biblical prophecy. This is only partly true. The eyes of the Jews will have to be opened, so they can acknowledge Jesus as their Messiah and Lord. This event is the next epochal event in history. Before it can happen, some Jews had to return to the land of Palestine. However the process by which this happened was probably not God's perfect plan. There are many prophecies in the Old Testament, but most speak of people returning in faith and in peace and blessing. These have not yet been fulfilled. We have not yet seen the real miracle that God promised. Ezekiel speaks of God's second best.

> In the latter years you will come into the land that is restored by the sword, whose inhabitants have been gathered from many nations to the mountains of Israel which had been a continual waste (Ezek 38:8).

This is not a return in peace and blessing, but a return "by the sword". The birth of the nation of Israel was accomplished by secular Jews using political and military power. It was the work of a well-organised nationalism rather than an act of God. The expansion of Israel has been accomplished by political alliances and military power. God allowed this to happen, because he can use all things for good, but that does not mean that this was his perfect plan.

The emergence of Israel had to happen so that God's greater purposes can be achieved, but we cannot assume that the timing of these events happened according to his ideal plan. They may have happened before God intended, so it is risky to turn the years 1948 or 1967 into markers for prophetic history.

## Jesus is Coming Soon

Another prophetic distraction is the belief that Jesus is coming soon. The odd thing is that Christians in every age have believed that they were living near the end of the world. For example, Martin Luther thought that Jesus would return during his lifetime. He was not alone in this view. It has been common since the days of the early church.

Looking at the whole of history, people who believed that Jesus was coming soon were wrong. That suggests that we should be careful assuming that Jesus is returning in our time. History shows that it is easier to be wrong than right about the time of Jesus return.

A belief that Jesus will return during the lifetime of our generation is quite arrogant. It assumes that we belong to a pivotal generation in the purposes of God. Judging by the western church, anyone suggesting that we are the peak of God's work on earth is deluded.

Humans can only see their own time in history clearly. Even the previous generation seems quite dim. Earlier generations fade into irrelevance. Our limited perspective means that we get deceived about our own importance. In contrast, God sees all generations from the same perspective. From his viewpoint, this generation may not be that important.

I believe that Jesus' return is thousands of years away. I will be ready, if I am proved wrong, but I do not believe that Jesus is coming soon. The scriptures contain thousands of prophecies that have not yet been fulfilled. These could not be fulfilled in one generation. Several Old Testament prophecies declare that the earth will be filled with the knowledge of the glory of Jesus. If such a glorious season were to last only a few years, it would not really be glorious. This glorious time could last for thousands of years.

This issue matters, because when Christians believe Jesus is coming soon, they fall into short-term thinking. Short-term thinking prevents people from investing in activities that will only bring benefits in future generations. This lack of long-term commitment has crippled the church and held back the Kingdom of God. Cultures that lose hope for the future collapse inwards and die. (For more on this topic see my book Times and Seasons).

# 12

# Prophets and Pastors

## The Prophetic is Essential

The prophetic ministry is not an optional extra. The church cannot survive and grow to maturity without it. The Bible is clear about the importance of the prophetic.

> Therefore, my brothers, be eager to prophesy, and do not forbid speaking in tongues (1 Cor 14:39).

> *Christianity is prophetic through and through. When the prophets are silent and the word of God is in short supply, the church withers and dies. If there are prophets today, their hands are tied and their mouths gagged by the clumsy democratic processes of church institutions. Prophecy is seldom heard within this establishment. For prophecy comes by the spirit of God and not by consensus or debate (Michael Harper).*

> *For our society to be renewed, it is necessary for the church, and by that I mean individual Christians together, to become a prophetic voice to our land. We must remember the price of being a prophet. If people were given the choice of straightening the wall or killing the prophet, they will usually kill the prophet instead of straightening the wall (Bob Mumford).*

A successful church will be one that appreciates the prophetic and allows prophets to develop in their ministry. A church without prophets will be a church with problems.

## No Heroes

We should not just be looking for a few heroic prophets like the men of the Old Testament. The outpouring of the Holy Spirit means that this gift has been distributed widely.

> In the last days, God says, I will pour out my Spirit on all people. Your sons and daughters will prophesy, your young men will see visions, your old men will dream dreams; Even on my servants, both men and women, I will pour out my Spirit in those days, and you will prophesy (Acts 2:17-18).

God wants prophets to be so numerous that there is at least one in every Christian fellowship. He would then be able to bring his word to the nation and the church, and the world.

## Prophets and Pastors

Every church needs a prophet and several pastor-teachers. The two ministries are complementary, but they have not always fitted together well. Pastors tend to be warm loving people. This is a strength for their ministry, but it means that they often find it hard to confront evil. They love to see people grow and to see the church united, so they can be tempted to compromise for the sake of peace and unity.

A prophet acts as a balance to this tendency. Prophets tend to see things in black and white and have a passion for holiness and truth. Their main concern is to see the church functioning according to the Word of God, but their zeal for purity and truth can make them appear to be hard and harsh. The pastors will temper their strictness and zeal with love and grace. And whereas pastors tend to concentrate on the present, the prophets give vision for the future.

Most modern churches are controlled by a pastor-manager and the bluntness of the prophet does not sit easily with them. If the pastor is insecure, he can be hurt by the prophet's words. The prophet seems to be a nuisance and life is easier if they leave.

The church needs both pastors and prophets to fully represent Christ. It must exhibit both the love and the holiness of God. Love without holiness is compromise. Holiness without love is harshness. If both ministries are present in a church then holiness and love will both be evident. The church will then be a true reflection of the character of God. Pastors and prophets need each other.

## Challenge to Pastors

Some pastors have been put off by bad experiences with unruly prophetic people, but this is not a good reason for rejecting the ministry. While some prophets have hurt people, the reality is that controlling pastors and inadequate pastoring have done far more damage to Christians.

In numerous situations, a whole church has fallen when their pastor has lost the plot. Pastors have far more power over people's lives than prophets. A pastor who gets lost can do far more harm than an over-zealous prophet. Where prophets have become unruly or controlling, the reason is usually inadequate or insecure leadership. Moreover, mature pastors have no reason to fear the prophetic. Wise pastors, who are loved by their flocks, can never be overcome or pushed aside by a prophet. Nevertheless, the bar of acceptance is set much higher for prophets.

*The questions is, why do we accept every other gift and calling among men with great failure and weakness? And yet, the ministry of the prophet who speaks hard truth is discounted with every excuse in the book (Kris Couchey - Bitter Prophets).*

Pastors have a key role in encouraging the development of the prophetic ministry. Those who are concerned about the damage that prophets could do should be more concerned about the effect of the lack of the prophetic on their church.

*Churches can survive without prophetic ministry, but they cannot be as healthy as they would without it (Tom Hamon – The Spirit of Wisdom and Revelation).*

The church will never reach its full potential without the ministry of the prophet, but the prophetic ministry will only be restored to fullness if there is a radical commitment from pastors to make it happen. The issue cannot be avoided. If pastors want to fully serve God, they will have to deal with the prophetic (and its problems). Here is a promise for pastors who are afraid of the prophetic.

Trust his prophets and you will succeed (2 Chron 20:20).

## Establishing Prophets in the Church

Most churches have no prophet to establish holiness and righteousness. They do not have a mature prophet to disciple young prophets, so God has had no choice but to develop young prophets in the wilderness. This is a second best option that produces many problems, but is the only way until the prophetic ministry is fully restored to the church.

This problem will have to be resolved by pastors. There is a surplus of pastors and a shortage of evangelists and prophets, which severely weakens the church. To correct the balance, pastors will have to take the initiative to restore prophets and evangelists to the church. Pastors without prophets in their churches could look in the wilderness for a growing prophet and seek to establish them in their ministry.

Obadiah protected, fed and sheltered the prophets when Jezebel was trying to destroy them (1 Kings 18:3-4). The modern church has an urgent need for Obadiahs.

*Many apostles and prophets today are not in church at all, because there is little room for them in traditional pastor-centred churches. They have been pushed to the side; they are often feared because they seem so strong, radical and different. Many have been not only marginalised but rejected, and as a result have given up on church almost completely, maybe with a last flicker and a spark of hope still burning in them (Wolfgang Simson - Houses That Changed the World).*

The prophetic ministry will only be restored to the church, if pastors are willing to take a risk with some who have been hurt and rejected. A good example of this is Paul, who began his ministry when Barnabas found him and brought him to Antioch (Acts 11:25-26). Barnabas demonstrated great courage, because Paul was a high-risk person, but his trust brought out the best in Paul. His commitment to Paul brought great blessing to the church.

Trust produces responsibility. Pastors will generally be surprised at how responsible prophets can be, if they are trusted. Prophets will be surprised at how open pastors can be, if the prophets commit to loving the pastors.

Because prophets sometimes speak hard words, pastors often assume that they need to be dealt with severely. They do not realise that under a brusque exterior, most prophets have a very sensitive spirit, which can easily be broken. They need a great deal of encouragement if they are to develop into their full ministry.

Pastors should encourage those in their church with prophetic gifts, even if they are a nuisance at times. They will eventually have prophets in their midst who can be trusted to speak the Lord's word. The more that pastors encourage the prophets, the better they will perform.

## Great Divide

Prophets are the people most likely to get a revelation of God's purposes and plans, but most pastors do not have relationship with a reliable prophet who can shed light in the darkness. We have a huge divide between the prophetic and the pastoral that prevents the church from fulfilling its ministry to the world.

Most churches are led by pastors who see intercessors and prophetic people as a problem and not a blessing. They assume that they will do more harm than good, if given too much freedom. Many pastors prefer to limit the prophetic to encouraging personal words to individual believers given in a church meeting where the process can be controlled.

This truncation of the prophetic role means that church leaders do not know how to handle a prophetic warning to a church, a city or a nation. When prophecy goes beyond the personal, they want to control the process. Some leaders have suggested that all words should be submitted to them for testing before being released. Yet, the same leaders say that they tend to ignore most of the prophecies given to them, because they are rubbish. That might be true, but it is hard to see how the prophetic role can emerge when the process is controlled by people who are ambivalent about prophecy.

The other side of this problem is that people with a prophetic calling have been squeezed out of church life and tend to live on the fringes where the battle is tougher, and isolation leaves them vulnerable to deception. Many have experienced rejection, leaving a residue of frustration and bitterness. When prophetic people gather together without a pastoral influence, they tend to become hard and judgmental, which tinges their words with a harshness that grates on everyone. This isolation and neglect leaves the church without a clear prophetic voice.

When the prophets are missing, the church gets chatter and confusion. Every church needs both pastors and prophets to function effectively. Until the prophetic role is integrated into the church, and the pastors and prophets come to unity through submission to each other, confusion will continue.

## Who is in Charge?

A serious argument is going on about authority in the church. Some people say that prophets do not need to submit to anyone, but God himself. Others say that everyone including the prophets must submit to a pastor. Still others say that apostles will govern the church and that pastors and prophets will both submit to the apostles. All these views are wrong. The Bible is quite clear.

> Submit to one another out of reverence for Christ (Eph 5:21).

Apostles, pastors, prophets and evangelists are not above this command. They are required to submit to each other out of respect for Jesus; just like all other Christians.

Instead of asking who is to govern and who is to submit to them, we should be looking for a model of church government that allows all the ministries to submit to each other, as required by Ephesians. Arguing about who should be in control will result in division and disunity.

Restoring prophets to the church will not work, if the pastors attempt to control the prophet. The challenge to the pastors is to say to the prophet, "We will submit to you, if you will submit to us". They will both have to trust each other and submit to each other. This will be risky for both the pastors and the prophet, but if they commit to it out of love for Jesus, great blessing will follow.

A church needs several pastors, at least one prophet and one evangelist to function effectively. There will only be unity if they are all submitted to each other. The prophet should submit to the pastors, but the pastors should also submit to the prophet. This will be hard, but fruitful.

Pastors, prophets and evangelists are very different from each other and are likely to have strong views about how things should be done. A great deal of love and trust will be required for them to submit to each other; but this should be normal for mature ministries. If the cross of Jesus is at work in their lives, it will be possible for these ministries to submit to each other.

Mutual submission among pastors, prophets and evangelists will be good for both them and the church. Their unity will provide balance and safety for the church. It would also be a marvellous testimony to the power of the gospel. On the other hand, if pastors and prophets cannot submit to each other, then there is something wrong with our gospel.

The biblical model for the leadership of the church is diversity of ministries submitted to each other. When evangelists gain control, a church becomes a revolving door. If prophets gain control, the church shrinks to a rigid righteous remnant. When pastors gain control, the church is soft and flabby. A healthy church needs each of these ministries submitting to each other in love.

Many church leaders are concerned about their members' lack of submission, yet they are unwilling to submit to others themselves. If the leaders of the church cannot submit to each other, then we should not be surprised if there is a lack of submission among less mature Christians.

## Persecution of Prophets

Prophets in the New Testament age will sometimes experience persecution and suffering. This happens when their message is not received, or when the church is resisting the Holy Spirit. However, when the church is functioning correctly, the prophet will be at peace with the church and just another ministry within it.

The treatment of prophets is a good test of the maturity of a church. When the church moves into apostasy, the prophets become more radical and drastic. In a mature church, prophets will be an integral part of the leadership.

## Prophetic Privilege

We must also be careful about building a theology of prophetic privilege. God has not promised to protect his prophets, but he will protect his word. Jesus warned that prophets would be persecuted. He did not promise they should be protected.

Prophets are often mistreated and mistrusted by the church. That has to change, but the solution is not to put prophets on a pedestal where they are immune from challenge. We want an environment where prophecy is welcomed, but vigorously tested and where prophetic ministries are respected, but rigorously assessed.

The idea that there are ministries, whether pastor or prophet, to whom we must blindly submit is wrong and dangerous. Too many Christians have been led off the right path, because they followed their pastor without questioning his decisions. We must not do the same with prophets.

The idea that prophets are subject only to prophets is wrong and dangerous. Prophets do have a role in testing judging prophecy (1 Cor 14:29), but that does not mean that others do not. Anyone receiving a prophecy has responsibility to test it and assess the prophet. Prophets can stir each other up into error. This happened in 1 Kings 22. Jehoshaphat was not a prophet, but he tested the court prophet's word and rejected their ministry.

## Developing Young Prophets

To a pastor, a young prophet can appear to be a particular nuisance. When first starting their ministry, prophets seem to be negative and overcritical. And because they are human they often make mistakes. Their intolerance and insensitivity can irritate the pastor. This causes the pastor to jump on the prophet, the first time that they make a mistake. The young prophet is often so crushed that they do not dare to prophesy again. The pastor is relieved because an apparent problem is gone. What the pastor does not realise is that a ministry that the church really needs has been squashed. Because this has happened so often, there is a shortage of prophets in the church.

At the same time, young prophets must learn to be patient, and allow God to develop their ministry. This will take time. Daniel was just a young man when he arrived in Babylon. He was middle aged when he received his first vision, and quite old when he received his greatest visions. Jeremiah was still prophesying when he was an old man.

Young prophets will only have partial vision. There will be times when they speak the Lord's word in the wrong spirit. God has to allow them to make mistakes so they can grow to maturity. They should not grasp at ministry, but wait on God to raise them up in due time. Those who humble themselves will be exalted.

Young prophets cannot emerge properly in a church that is led by a pastor alone. (The same applies to evangelists). Pastors cannot disciple budding prophets effectively. The young prophet will either start challenging the pastor and become a nuisance, or will be stifled by the pastor and lose their cutting edge. A young prophet will develop best in a church where the pastors and a prophet are in submission to each other. The young prophet will be drawn to the other prophet to learn how to function in their gifting. They will also be able to learn how to relate to a pastor.

When young prophets need correction, they will generally receive it better from the other prophets in their church. They will need frequent correction and will sometimes need to be corrected very firmly. This is best done by a more mature prophet whom they respect.

On the other hand, when a young prophet is treated harshly by the senior prophet or becomes discouraged as often happens, they will need and appreciate the comfort and encouragement of their pastor. Young prophets should develop a healthy relationship with the pastors and prophets in their church. If they can grow within these relationships, they will be less likely to wander off into isolation.

## Judge Carefully

When a prophet speaks publicly, the pastors in their church have responsibility to assess the word and decide if it is right and true. We need more rigorous debate about some of the words that are spoken by prophets.

On the other hand, pastors should be very careful about attacking a prophet in the wrong spirit. These attacks can be a way of rejecting words that God is speaking to them. If the word is true, they are putting themselves in a dangerous position. Rejecting God's word is risky for pastors, as it leaves their flock vulnerable to spiritual attack. The pastor critiquing a prophecy must keep their heart right. They must not speak out of envy or jealousy.

## Financial Support

The prophet's loyalty to God must take priority over their loyalty to the church. While being sufficiently involved to know what is going on, they must be detached enough to be objective. This means that a prophet should not be a paid officer of the church. It is interesting that Paul says that gifts of money should only be given to those elders who work hard at teaching or preaching (1 Timothy 5:17). That is, only pastor-teachers and evangelists should receive financial support. Prophets are not included because being a prophet is not full-time work. They can work part time to support themselves. A prophet who is financially independent will not be tempted to compromise.

# 13

# Prophetic Message

The primary message of the prophets is the person and character of God. Most problems in the church and the world are rooted in an incorrect or unbalanced view of God. Prophets will consistently speak of his love, mercy, righteousness, holiness, sovereignty and justice.

> *Prophecy always calls for a faith response. God never gives opinions; he gives orders (Tom Marshall- The Coming of the Prophets).*

> *We need to get a prophetic vision of the church; to see the church as God sees it (John Brook).*

The second part of the prophetic message will be God's plan for history. Prophets describe what God is doing in the world. They give the long-term plan and announce future events, explaining how they fit into the long-term plan.

> This is the plan determined for the whole world; this is the hand stretched out over all nations. For the Lord Almighty has purposed, and who can thwart him? His hand is stretched out, and who can turn it back (Is 14:26-27)?

The goal is the Kingdom of God. Prophets should be obsessed with the Kingdom. They should have a passion to see the Kingdom of God become a reality on earth.

*What did the prophets prophesy? Inclusively, they prophesied concerning the King and the Kingdom (T. Austin-Sparks - Prophetic Ministry).*

## God's Word is Powerful and Effective

The word that comes from God will be effective.

> God is not a man, that he should lie, nor a son of man, that he should change his mind. Does he speak and then not act? Does he promise and not fulfil (Num 23:19)?

God will fulfil his word.

*The church has been unable to give an effective lead in secular society due to the loss of a sense of mission and direction. Without a clear sense of its own purpose, identity and destiny the church has been powerless to influence an increasingly secular society. A major cause of the church's loss of direction has been due to the lack of a clear concept of the meaning of history. Mankind is crying out for an understanding of history. This is of fundamental importance for grappling with the underlying issues concerning the meaning and purpose of life itself. The church will never be able to satisfy the deepest longings of mankind and give a lead to secular nations or point the way to creative policies promoting health, happiness and the well-being of mankind until Christians recover an understanding of history (Clifford Hill - Shaking the Nations).*

*Repentance and practical holiness are based on a word concerning the future; the vision of wrath to come is the basis of a present seeking of the mercy of God; the vision of bliss to come is a call to a walking in the light now (J A Motyer - Prophets and Prophecy).*

*The Bible reveals a God who has plans for the whole world, which cannot be thwarted. Once God has announced his purposes nothing can stand against him or prevent him from fulfilling his word. This understanding of God as the Lord of history is something that has very largely been lost by the western church. It has resulted in a powerlessness to declare the word of God with prophetic power and conviction in the second half of the twentieth century when all the nations have been shaken. When God stretches out his hand and says that the time has come for a nation or a people, they can no longer stand (Clifford Hill - Shaking the Nations).*

## About the Author

Ron McKenzie is a Christian writer
living in Christchurch, New Zealand.
During the 1980s, he served as
the pastor of a church,
but found that he did not fit that role.
He is now employed as an economist
and writes in his spare time.
He is married with three adult children.

# By the Same Author

## Being Church Where We Live

This challenging book offers a radical vision for the church that will stir hearts and provide guidance for people living through the Time of Distress and preparing for the glory of the Kingdom.

## Times and Seasons

This book takes a different approach to God's plan for history. It begins with the ministry of Jesus and the sending of the Holy Spirit and ends with the glory of the Kingdom of God. The key seasons and the epochal events that mark the change from each season to the next are clearly described.

## Healing: Insights for Christian Elders

Healing the sick was crucial for the success of the early church. The modern Christian practice falls far short of their experience. This book provides fifteen keys that will help God's people obtain greater victory over pain and sickness.

# Coming Soon

## The Government of God

The Kingdom of God is one of the greatest themes of the Bible. This book will explain how the government of God can transform economic and social life.

Made in the USA
San Bernardino, CA
28 August 2017